GRÀFICA
DE LES
RAMBLES
THE SIGNS OF BARCELONA
LOUISE FILI

PRINCETON ARCHITECTURAL PRESS

NEW YORK

GRÀFICA DE LES RAMBLES

THE SIGNS OF BARCELONA

LOUISE FILI

PUBLISHED BY PRINCETON ARCHITECTURAL PRESS · A McEvoy Group company · New York, New York 10003 · 202 Warren Street · Hudson, New York 12534 · 37 East Seventh Street · New York, New York · Visit our website at www.papress.com. © 2017 Louise Fili Ltd.

SPECIAL THANKS TO Janet Behning, Nolan Boomer, Nicola Brower, Abby Bussel, Erin Cain, Tom Cho, Barbara Darko, Benjamin English, Jenny Florence, Jan Cigliano Hartman, Susan Hershberg, Lia Hunt, Mia Johnson, Valerie Kamen, Simone Kaplan-Senchak, Jennifer Lippert, Kristy Maier, Sara McKay, Eliana Miller, Wes Seeley, Rob Shaeffer, Sara Stemen, Paul Wagner, and Joseph Weston of Princeton Architectural Press —Kevin C. Lippert, publisher.

EDITOR Sara Stemen · DESIGNERS Louise Fili, Nicholas Misani, Raphael Geroni · COVER DESIGNERS Louise Fili and Rachel Michaud/Louise Fili Ltd.

GLOBAL CONSULTANT Jordi Duró · GLOBAL CONSULTANT Carla Cimino · RESEARCH ASSISTANT Odette Cimino · COPYRIGHT PAGE CONSULTANT Nicholas Misani.

INTRODUCCIÓ

ON MY FIRST TRIP TO BARCELONA, IN THE EARLY 1970s, I WAS ENCHANTED BY Modernisme, the city's own brand of art nouveau, which had influenced the entire urban landscape. Antoni Gaudí's elegant architecture was intoxicating—and then there was the shop signage: fluid and poetic, enhanced by mosaics, gold leaf, stained glass, and wrought iron. It was love at first sight.

My previous books on European signage were created out of a sense of urgency; I felt compelled to record the beautiful street typography of Italy and Paris before it would vanish forever. After *Grafica della Strada* and *Graphique de la Rue*, Barcelona seemed like the obvious next choice, especially given reports of its signage disappearing at an alarmingly rapid rate. There was no time to wait for my publisher to say yes: I spent hours on Google Street View, plotted out my maps, and left as quickly as possible.

I arrived in late December and literally *ran* to my favorite spots, fearing they might be bare. One of the signs I was most looking forward to seeing was Fotos López, a lovely script that I had admired in photographs. I raced to the location to find an empty facade, with only the ghostly traces of typography left behind. I was devastated; I seemed to have missed the removal by a matter of minutes. The next day, when interviewed by a reporter from *El País*, I happened to mention the incident, which was in turn noted in the article that appeared a day later. The following week, after I returned to New York, I received an email from Angel López, grandson of the Fotos López founder. He wrote that he and his family were very moved by the article and added, "If you are ever back in Barcelona we can remount the sign on the wall for you to take a picture." I returned as soon as I was able (how long could an offer like that last?), and the entire López family came out for the event—including Angel's sister Rosa with her husband and three children, who had made the trip from Germany. The photo studio had closed a year before, and although the family still owns the building, concerns about theft (a frequent subject in Barcelona) had kept the sign safely indoors. This book is dedicated to the López family, who, along with many other small businesses, have managed to keep the city's exquisite historic signage alive.

MODERNISTA

ODERNISME, THE LABEL GIVEN TO AN ART AND LITERATURE MOVEMENT AT THE turn of the century, was centered in Barcelona and included many of the decorative arts (cabinetmaking, carpentry, wrought iron, ceramic tiles, glassmaking, silver- and goldsmith work), which were particularly significant, especially as an adjunct to architecture. Although it was part of a general trend that emerged in Europe (art nouveau in France and Belgium, Jugendstil in Germany, Secession in Austria-Hungary, Stile Liberty in Italy, and Glasgow Style in Scotland) from roughly 1888 (the first Barcelona world's fair) to 1911, in Catalonia the style found its own unique personality, and much of it is still preserved in the shop signage today.

El Indio (pages 14–17), the opulent shop for fabrics, opened its doors in 1870, during a time when naming shops for assumed exotic ancestry was in vogue. In 1922 architect Vilaró i Valls gave his lush Modernista imprimatur to this corner facade, with luminous gold-leaf typography listing the shop's various offerings: *lanerias*, *sederias*, *novedades* (woolens, silks, the latest). Known to have been frequented by the surrealist painter Salvador Dalí, the shop also included a larger-than-life-sized automated wooden Indian. Sadly, El Indio closed in 2014, although it is now on the *llistat d'edificis emblemàtics protegits* (list of protected shopfronts) maintained by the Ajuntament de Barcelona.

The Antigua Casa Figueras (pages 12–13) traces its beginnings to a pasta factory in 1842. The shop was designed by architect Manuel Joaquim Raspall—who also crafted Casa Texidor (pages 10–11). In 1902 painter Antoni Ros i Güell decorated the shop inside and out, with unique mosaic work by the Italian artisan Mario Maragliano (pages 144–45)—quite suitable for its current life as a chocolate shop.

Modernisme has left an indelible mark on a number of *farmàcies* throughout Barcelona. Farmàcia Bolós (pages 19–21), designed in 1902 by architect Antoni de Falguera i Sivilla, is a prime example, with its large, wood-trimmed, leaded-glass entrance festooned with an orange tree design. Inside, the original botanical-inspired friezes are still intact. Farmàcia Puigoriol by architect Marià Pau (pages 24–25) features equally distinctive lettering in gold leaf and still maintains its original gas lamps.

FARMACIA

Farmácia
BOLÓS

SECCION H

MOSAICOS

TERRAZOS

PAN
de
CASTILLA

PANADERIA
DE LA CONCEPCIÓN

PAN
De LUJO

11 M. BOUE 11

CAMISERIA PONS

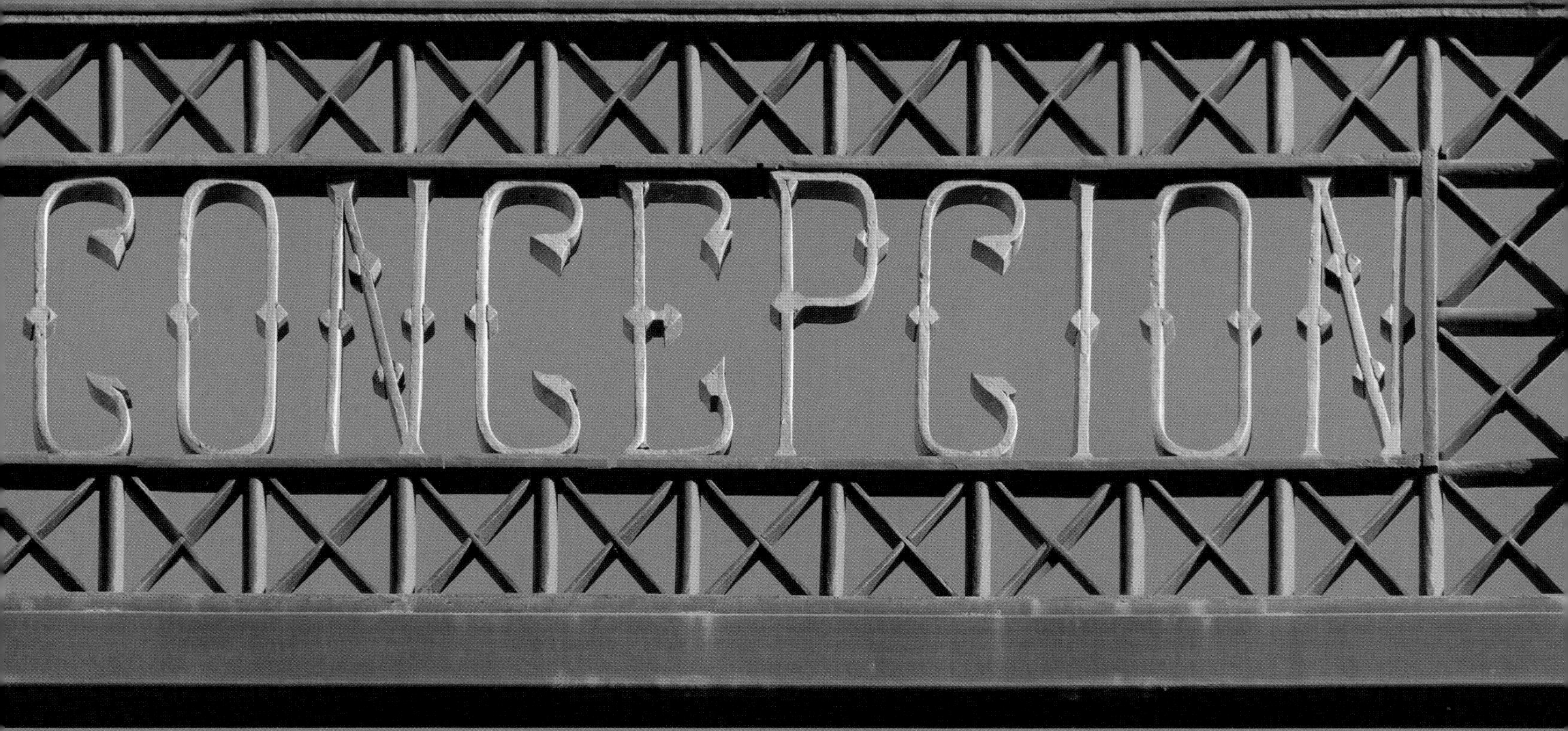
CONCEPCION

ZAPATERIA LA

LIBRERIA

MANTELERIA

AMPURDANESA

A.G. TALLERS 3

VIOLA

NOVEDADES

ART DECO

EVENTUALLY, MODERNISME'S NATURALISTIC MOTIFS GAVE WAY TO ART DECO'S SEDUCTIVE geometric patterns and smoother, sleeker lines. Introduced at a world's fair held in Paris in 1925, art deco, characterized by streamlined compositions and a sophisticated, machine-age look, arrived in Spain by way of Barcelona, where the style still thrives—from corset shops (page 72, top) to mattress stores (pages 82–83, top).

A walk along the Rambla de Canaletes, just below the Plaça de Catalunya, reveals several deco gems: Restaurant Nuria (pages 74–75 and opposite), with its graceful yet simple rounded letterforms; Farmàcia Nadal (pages 46–47), which features a stylish corner facade built in 1917 (although the wording has changed in a number of variations, the deco treatment of "Farmàcia" has remained intact); and Boadas (page 56), Barcelona's oldest cocktail bar.

Just a little farther is Escribà. Many memorable signs (pages 66–67) adorn this much-admired chocolate shop, which stylistically runs the gamut from Modernista (pages 144–45) to deco. Escribà's other location (pages 76–77) features a more modern take on deco, although it is still unique. Sadly, those signs were removed shortly after I photographed them.

Deco signage is never short on surprises. Despojos Buey-Ternera (pages 78–79) at the Mercat d'Hostafrancs is one of the most unusual signs for a butcher shop. The decorative flowers in the type and border almost neutralize the wording (fortunately), which roughly translates as "Remains of Oxen and Calves." The dramatic, curved 1939 sign for Lampisteria y Electricidad Espuñes (pages 52–53), with painted wooden letters, is much more than one would expect from an electrician's shop, particularly with the inventive style of the tilde symbol. And the oversized sign for Conservatori Femení (page 64) pays tribute to the only music school for women, and the only female orchestra that regularly worked in Spain in the twentieth century.

The corner sign for Santa Eulàlia (page 61) makes use of the original logo design from 1926 for this haute couture shop for women. Look carefully around the storefront and you'll notice two other completely different versions of the logo. (The original is by far the best.)

47

FERRETERIA
GRANJA
JUAN TEMPRADO

METALLISTERIA
VENDRELL
BOLIBAR

49

APO

DROG

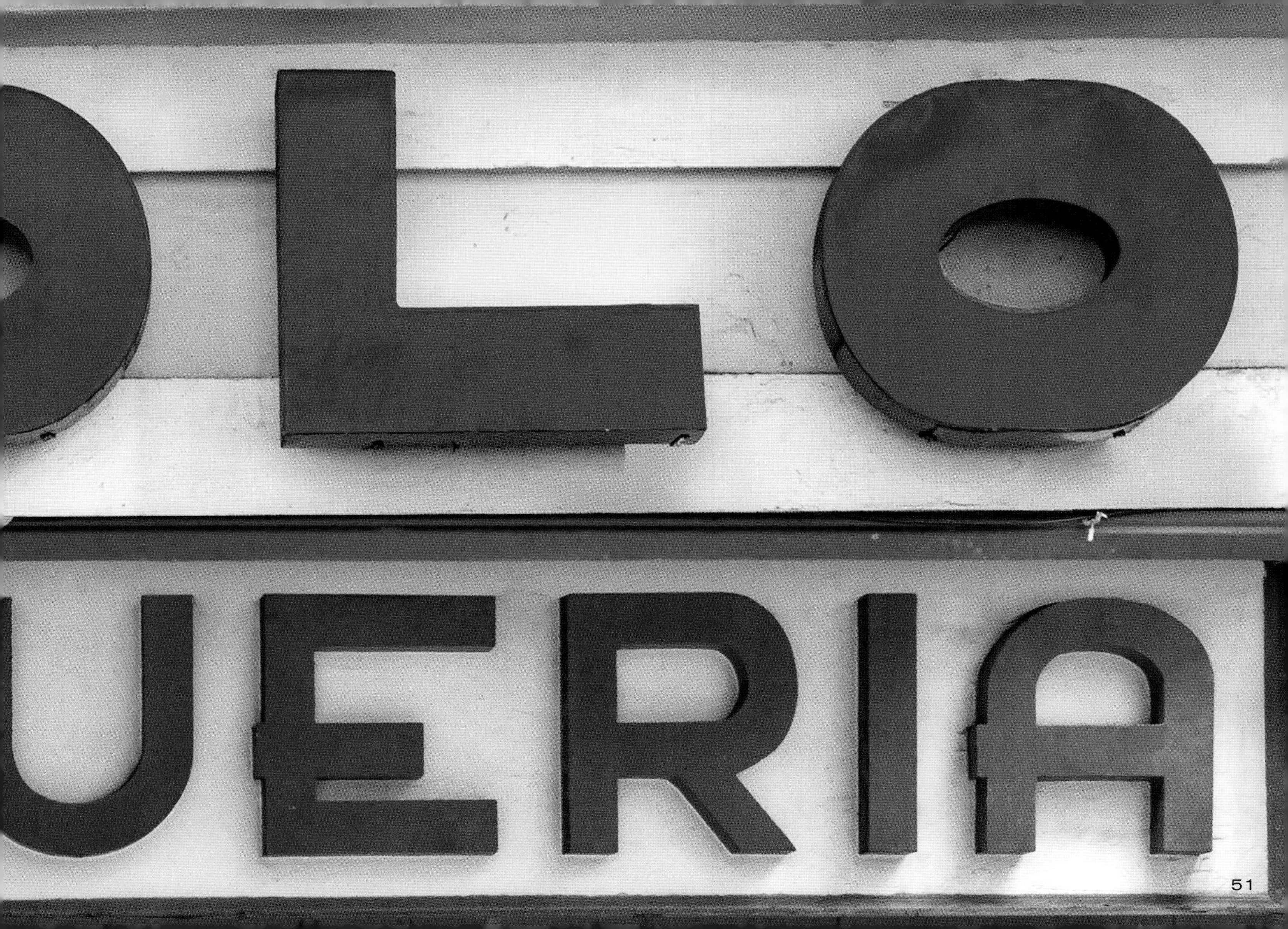
LO
UERIA

LAMPISTERIA
ELECTRICIDA

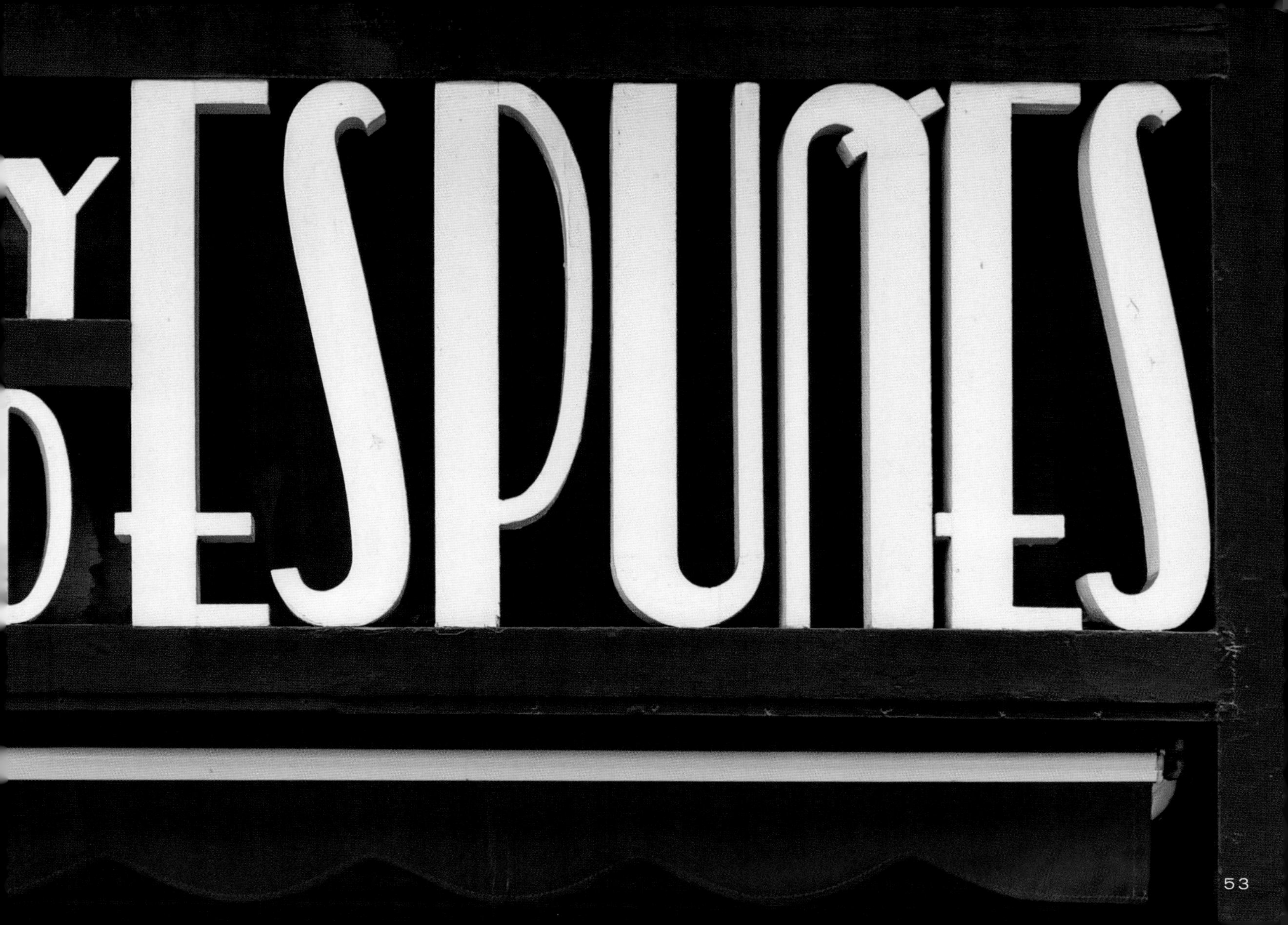
ESPUNES

J.MU

GRAN

RRIA

A PUY

56

ELS TRE

FARMÀCIA

JULIÀ

S TOMBS

COLMADO

ACHS

59

A. BALLARIN

36 TOCINERIA

RICARDO

BAR PASTIS

TINTORERIA

SANTA SANTA
EULALIA EULALIA

CONSERVATORI
FEMENÍ
SOLFEIG · PIANO
ARMONIA
CANT · VIOLÍ
VIOLONCEL
ARPA · GUITARRA
MANDOLINA
RÍTMICA
IDIOMES

JUAN ANTONIO

NADAL GIRO

F. LARAUZA
ACADEMIA CENTRAL
DE CORTE

65

CROMO
INDUS
BALMES DOS·CE

DURO

TRIAL

VUITANTA·U

CHOCOLAT

BRE

CARAMELOS

ES · GRAGEAS

TON

· CONSERVAS

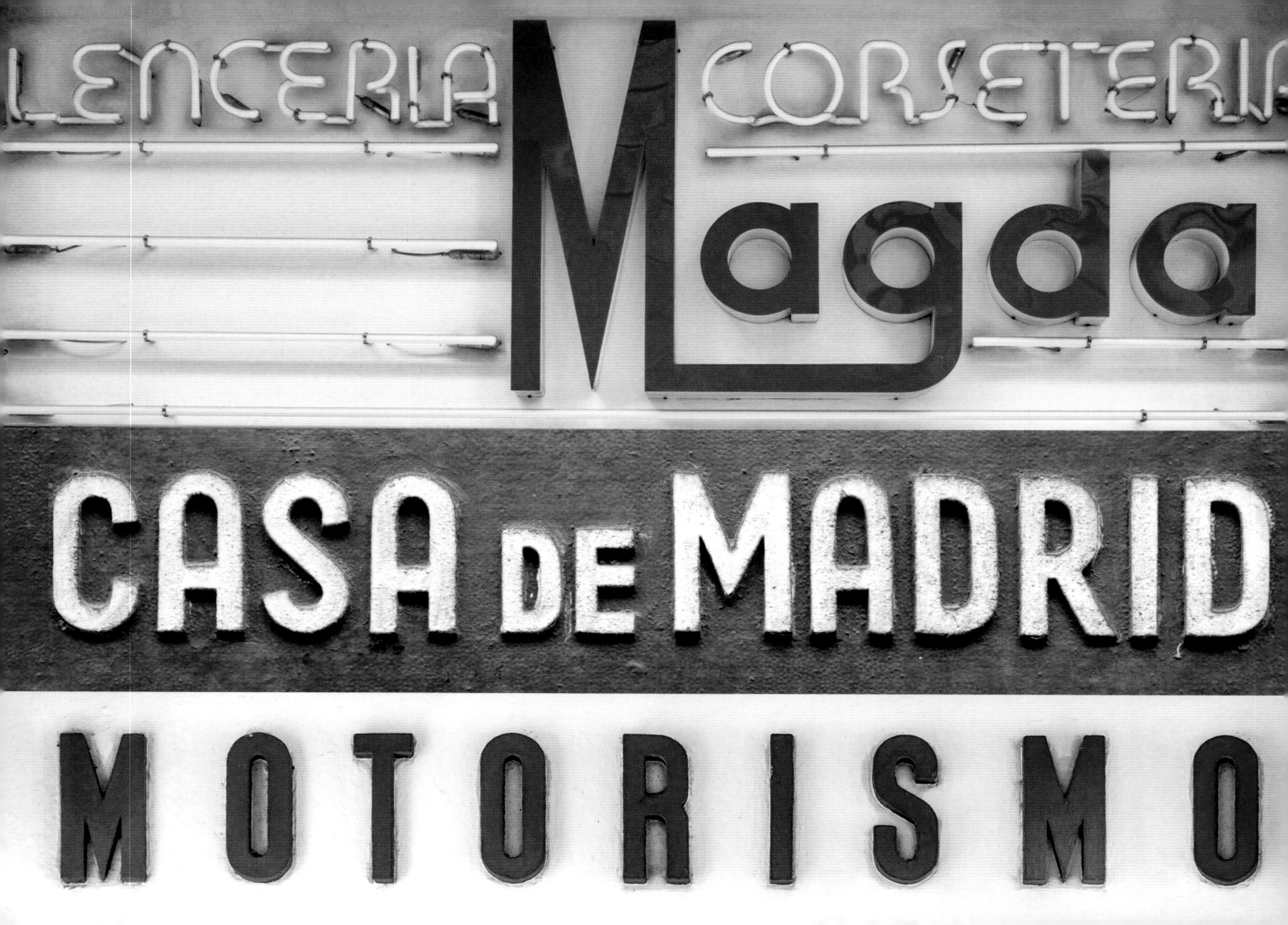
LENCERIA
Magda
CORSETERIA
CASA DE MADRID
MOTORISMO

FARMÀCIA

JAMONES MATAS

XARCUTERIA

RESTAURAN

N U

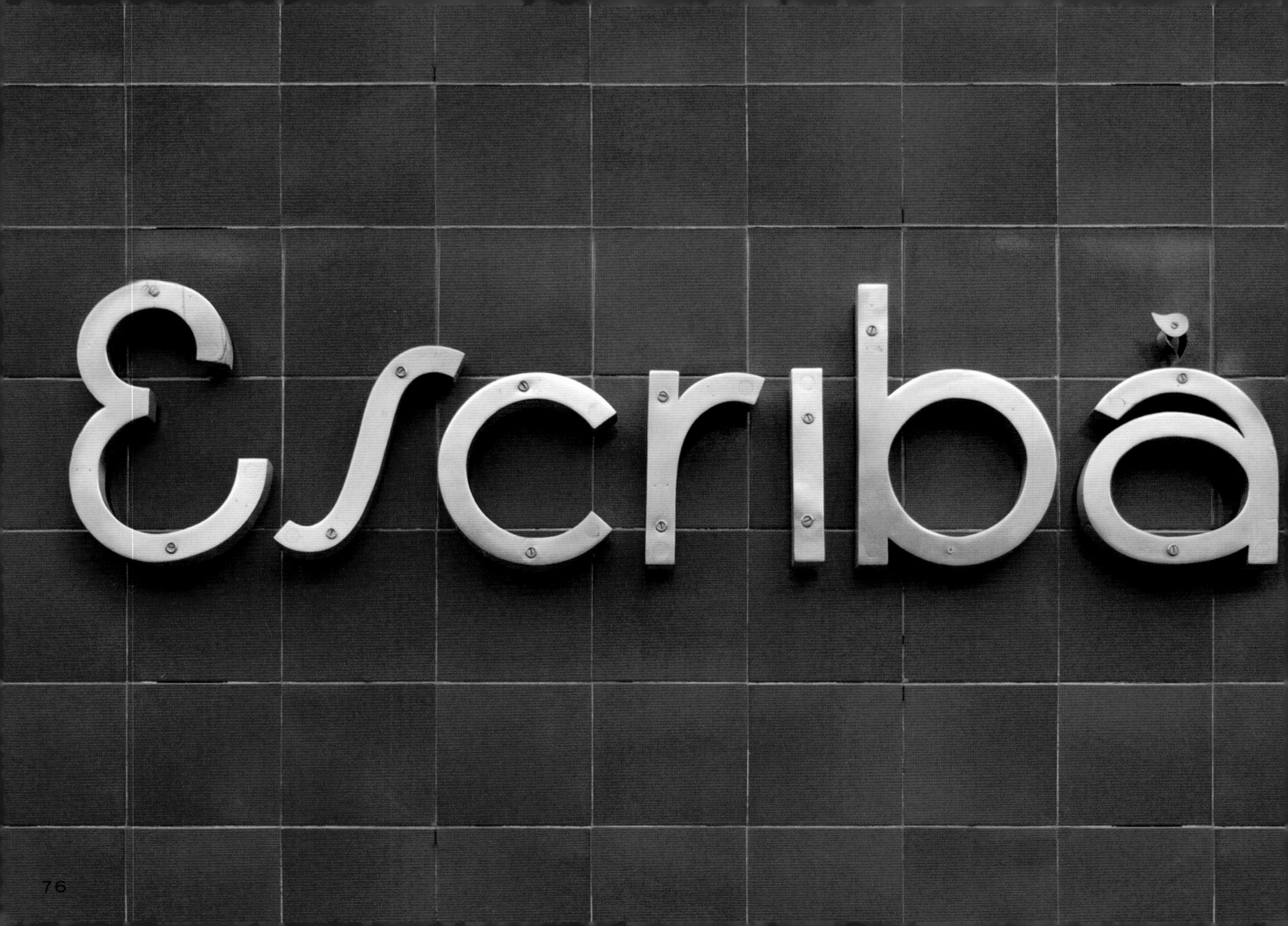
Escribà

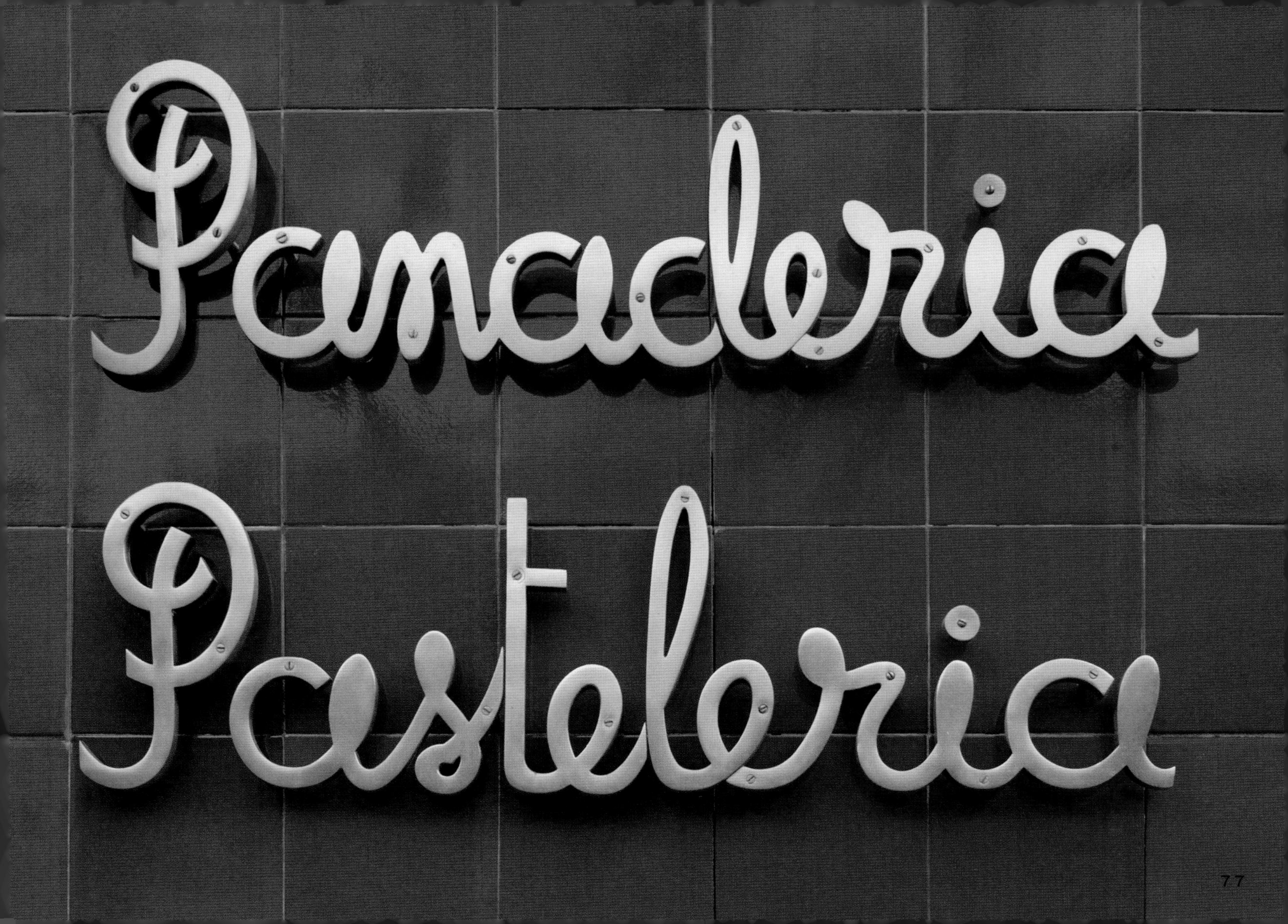
Panaderia
Pasteleria

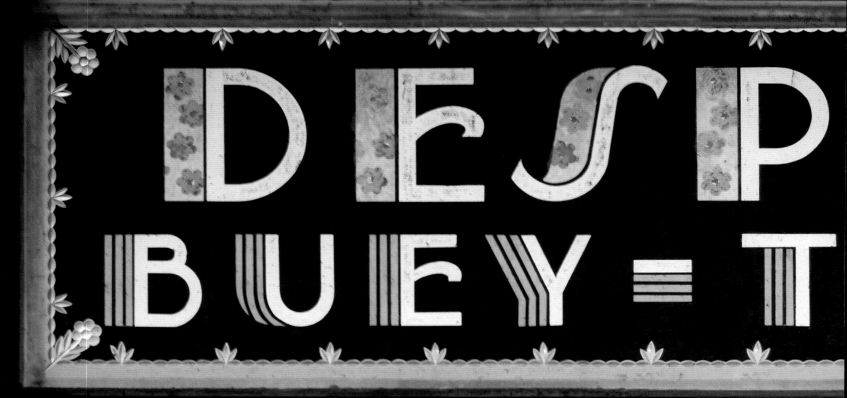

OJOS

ERNERA

oca

153

SALA DALMAU

LAMPI

MARTI R

GALERIA D'ART

OTERIA

pinteria

MOTA D

AMAYA

RESTAURANT

ESCANS

ALFA

CURSIVA

BARCELONA SCRIPTS COVER THE SPECTRUM FROM HYPER-ELEGANT TO THE EVERYDAY. From the classic grace of gold-leaf cursives for Casa Gispert (page 128) and Granja M. Viader (page 129) to the more playful interpretations crafted in neon (Giardinetto Restaurant, page 89), each is memorably beautiful.

Fotos López (pages 92–93) is an undeniable favorite, due not only to its singular backstory (page 6), but also as the last remaining classic sign for a photographer's studio in Barcelona. This style of angled script, finished with a dramatic swash, served to brand many studios in Europe as well as the United States in the early twentieth century, and could often be found in the lower right corner of matted photographs.

La Selecta (pages 106–7) and El Trèbol (pages 116–17) both are *mercerias*, but they communicate their message in different ways—each an equally grand rendition for a store selling threads and buttons. El Molino, El Rei del Calçat, and El Corte Inglés (page 98), all dimensional, have a spirited timelessness.

A gracefully arched Farmàcia sign (pages 86–87) is the perfect complement to the lacy gingerbread-like cutouts that adorn one facade. A red cross and building numbers are all carefully considered framed additions to this shopfront design.

At the Mercat de l'Abaceria Central (page 109), scripts enhance signage for eggs and fresh fish. As these market signs disappear with increasing frequency throughout Barcelona, one appreciates the few that still remain.

Wrought iron and script make a perfect pairing; Villa Emilia and El Refugi (pages 118 and 119) near Tibidabo, the mountain that overlooks Barcelona, feature eye-catching upright scripts crafted in metal and mounted onto stucco facades. Sedó (pages 124–25) takes a more angular approach, giving wrought iron a stylish yet slightly menacing look.

The emblematic Bella Aurora (opposite and pages 120–21) is a graceful cursive suspended above a one-story building that is now a travel office. The sign can be viewed from many vantage points, although I prefer the earth tones of the buildings as a backdrop, juxtaposed with the celestial blue of the script—essentially a reverse of the normal figure/ground.

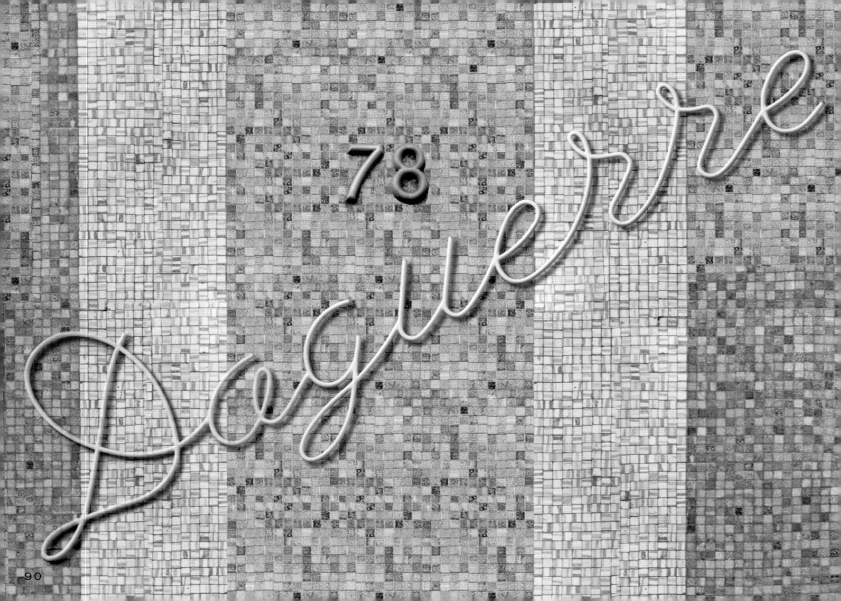

talleres elec

Pastelería

Control G

romecanicos

Bomboneria

ma Sellos

Sebastián Ca
Tejidos y
Pesca

orla Martín

onfecciones

Salada

El Molino

El Rei del calçat

El Corte Inglés

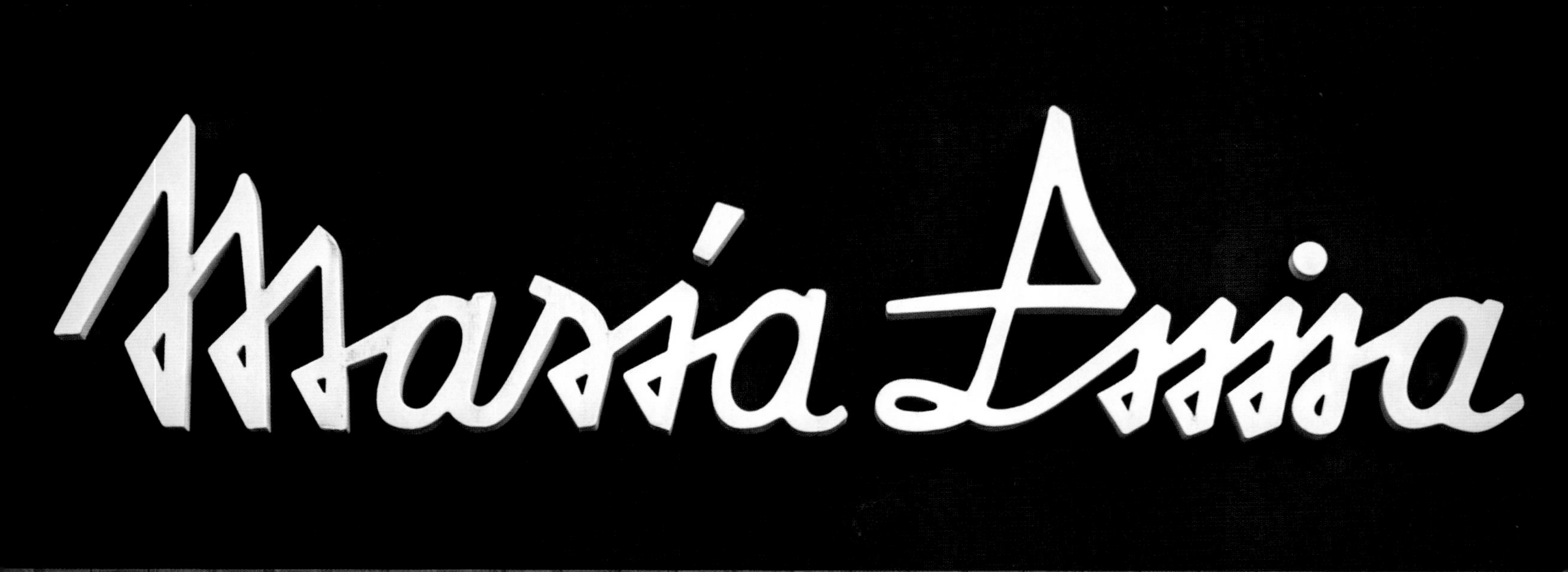

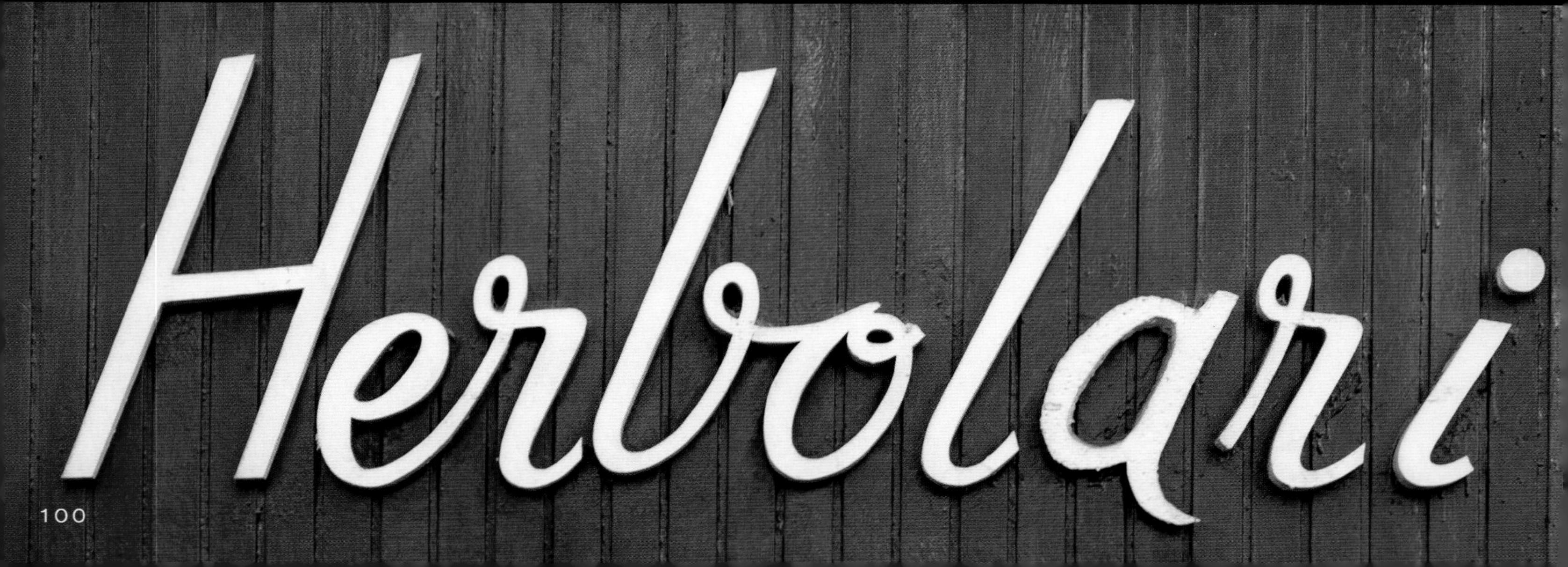
Herbolari

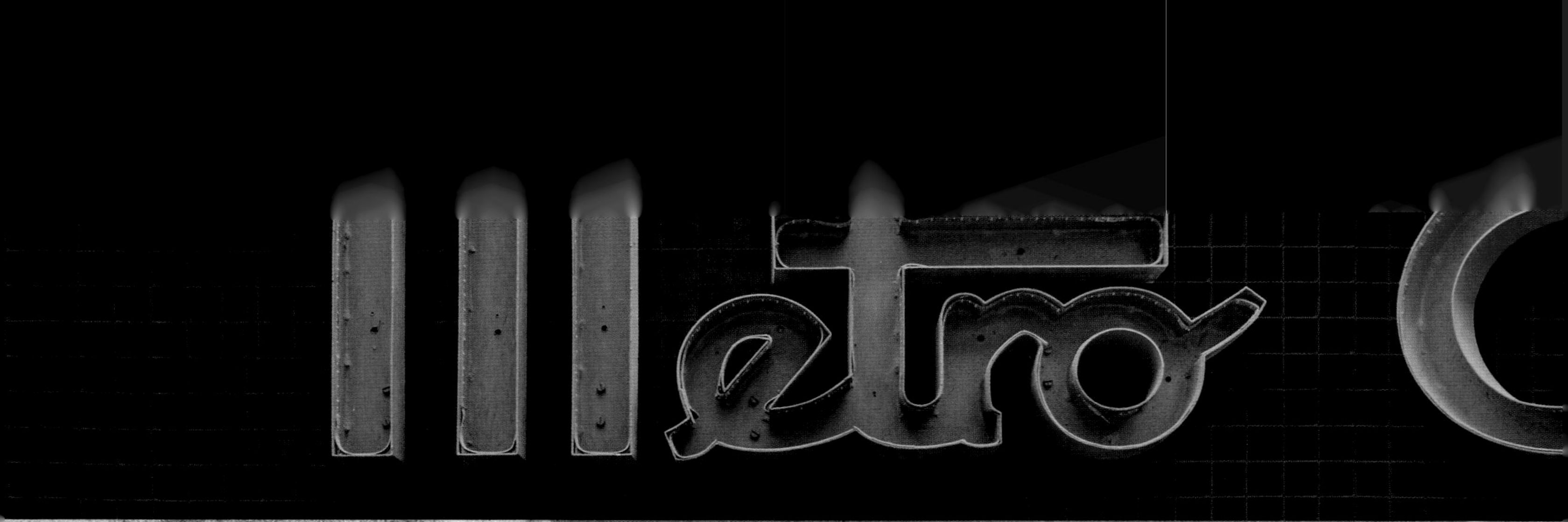
Metro

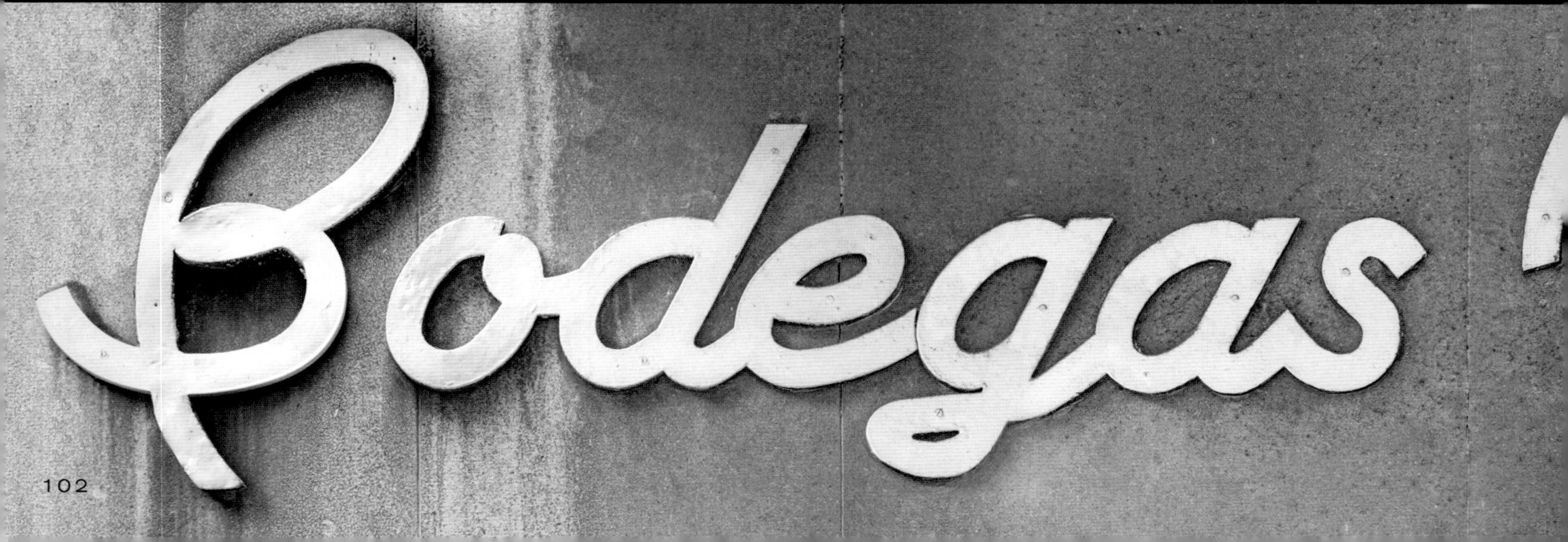
Bodegas

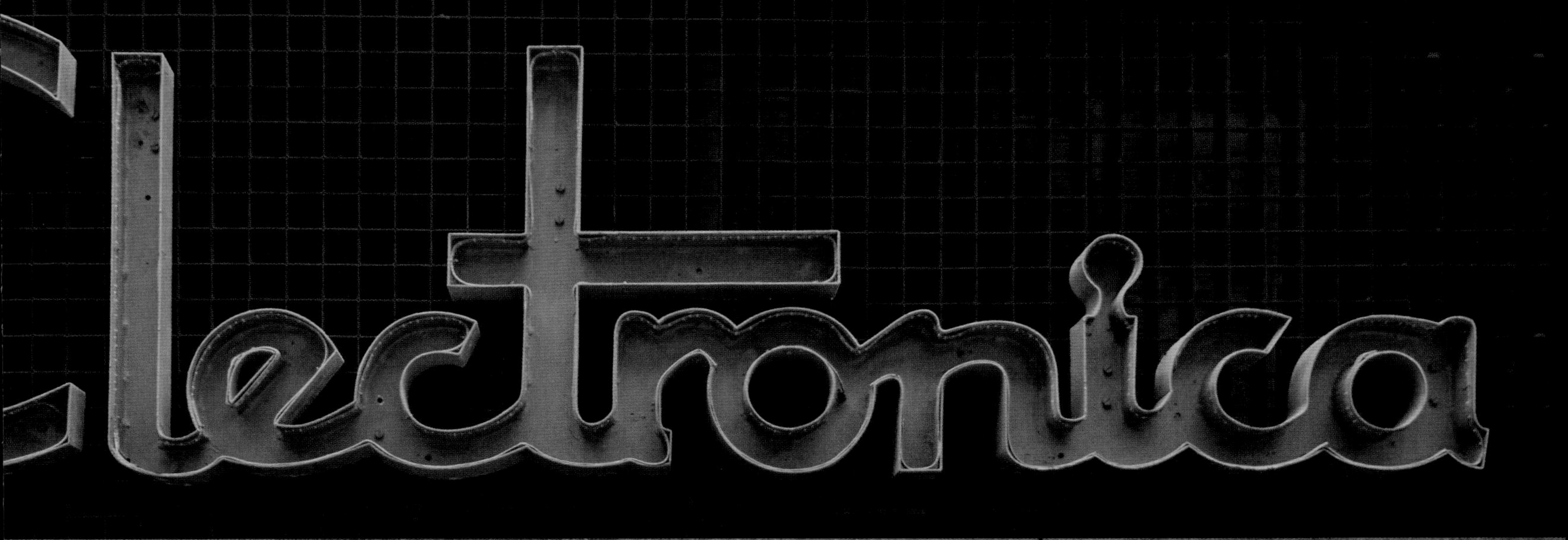
lectronica

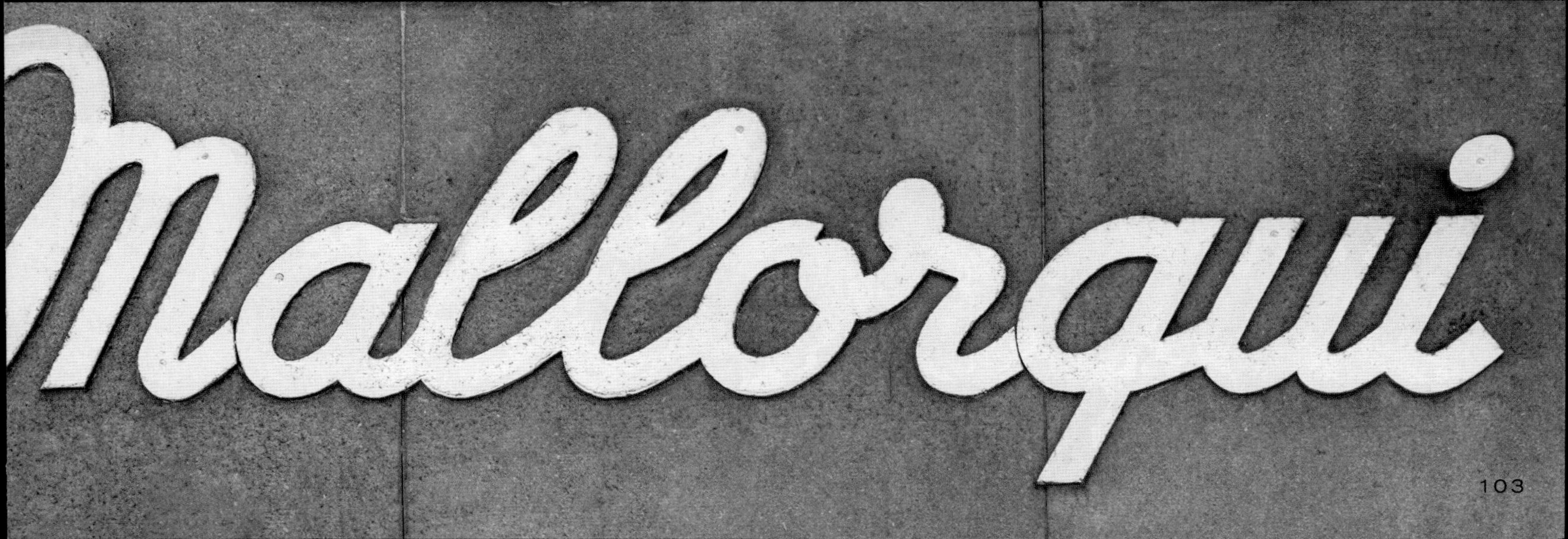
Mallorqui

Perfumeria *Medias* Merceria

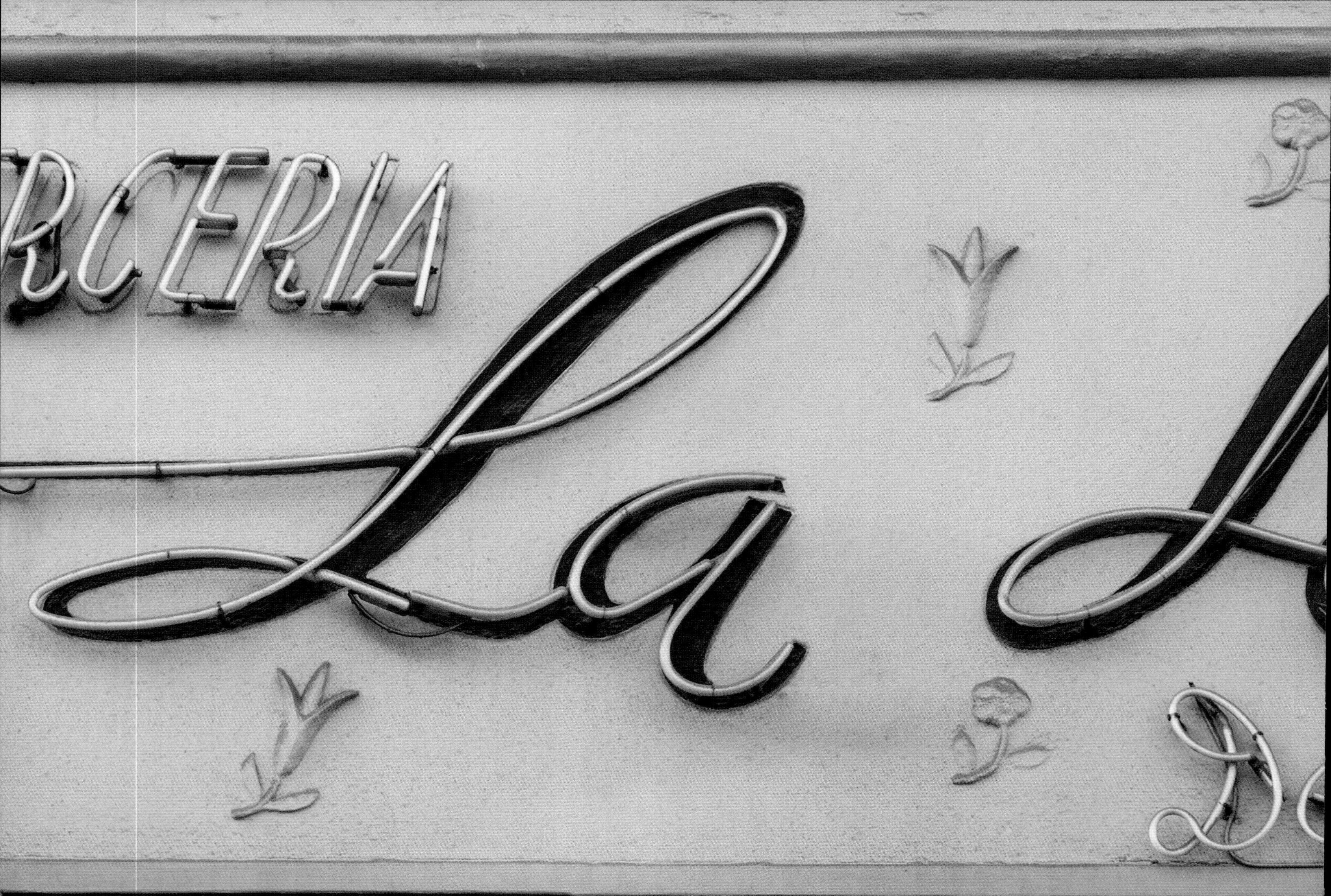
RCERIA
La

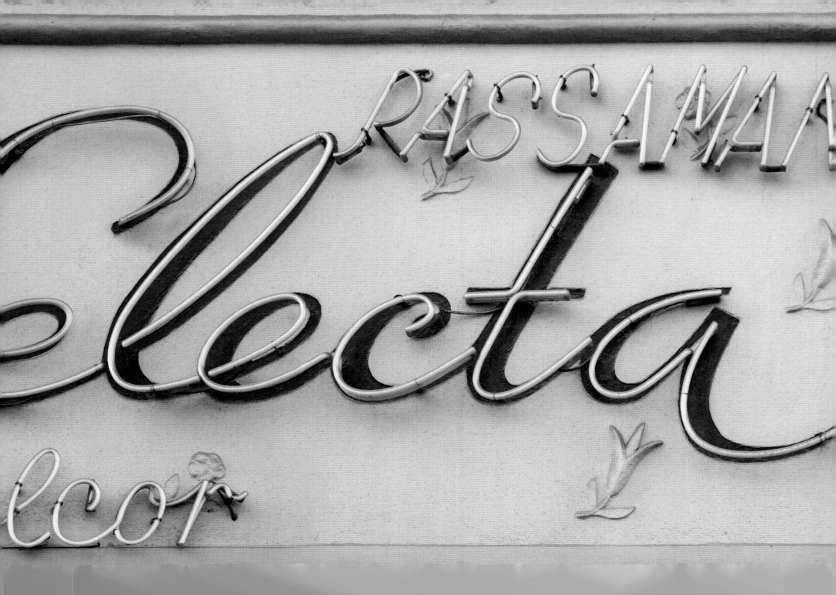

Paquita

Huevos

Pescado Fresco

COLCHONERIA
Lider

Ligilsa

WALKIFLOR

Forné

FLORS ARTIFICIALS

Estivill

PASTISSERIA Bonet

Estilográfica

RuizOrtega

opticos

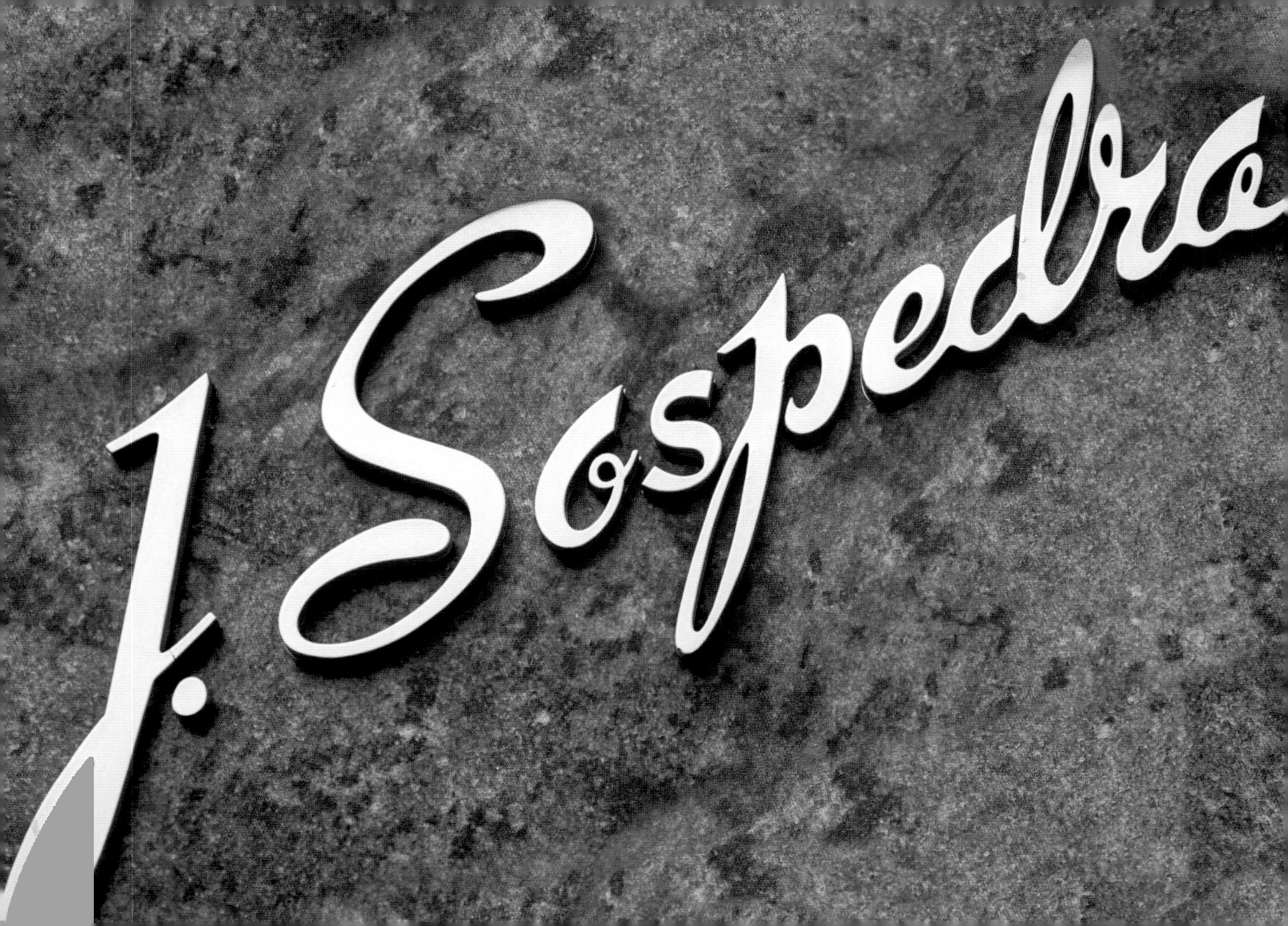
J. Sospedra

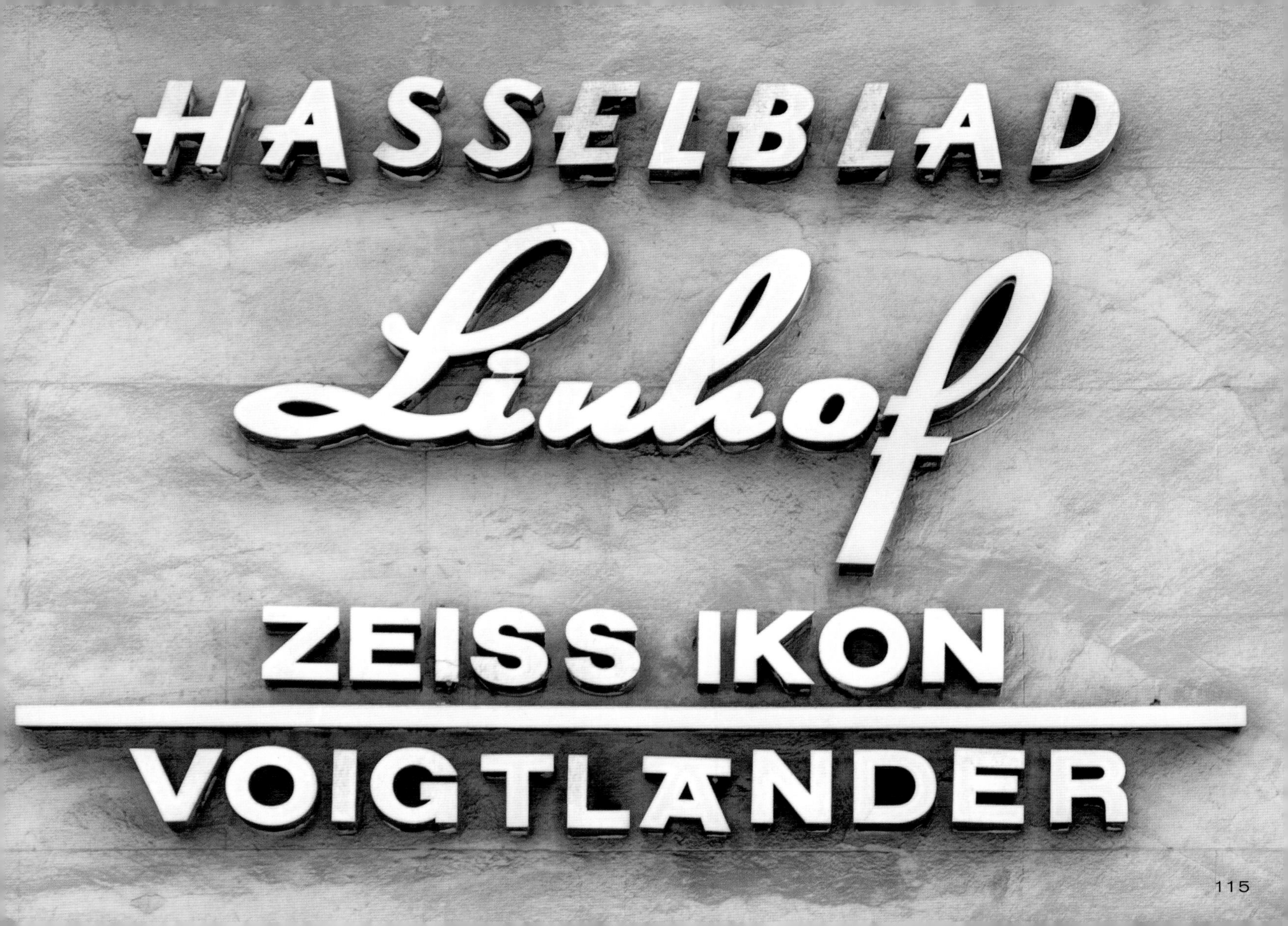
HASSELBLAD
Linhof
ZEISS IKON
VOIGTLÄNDER

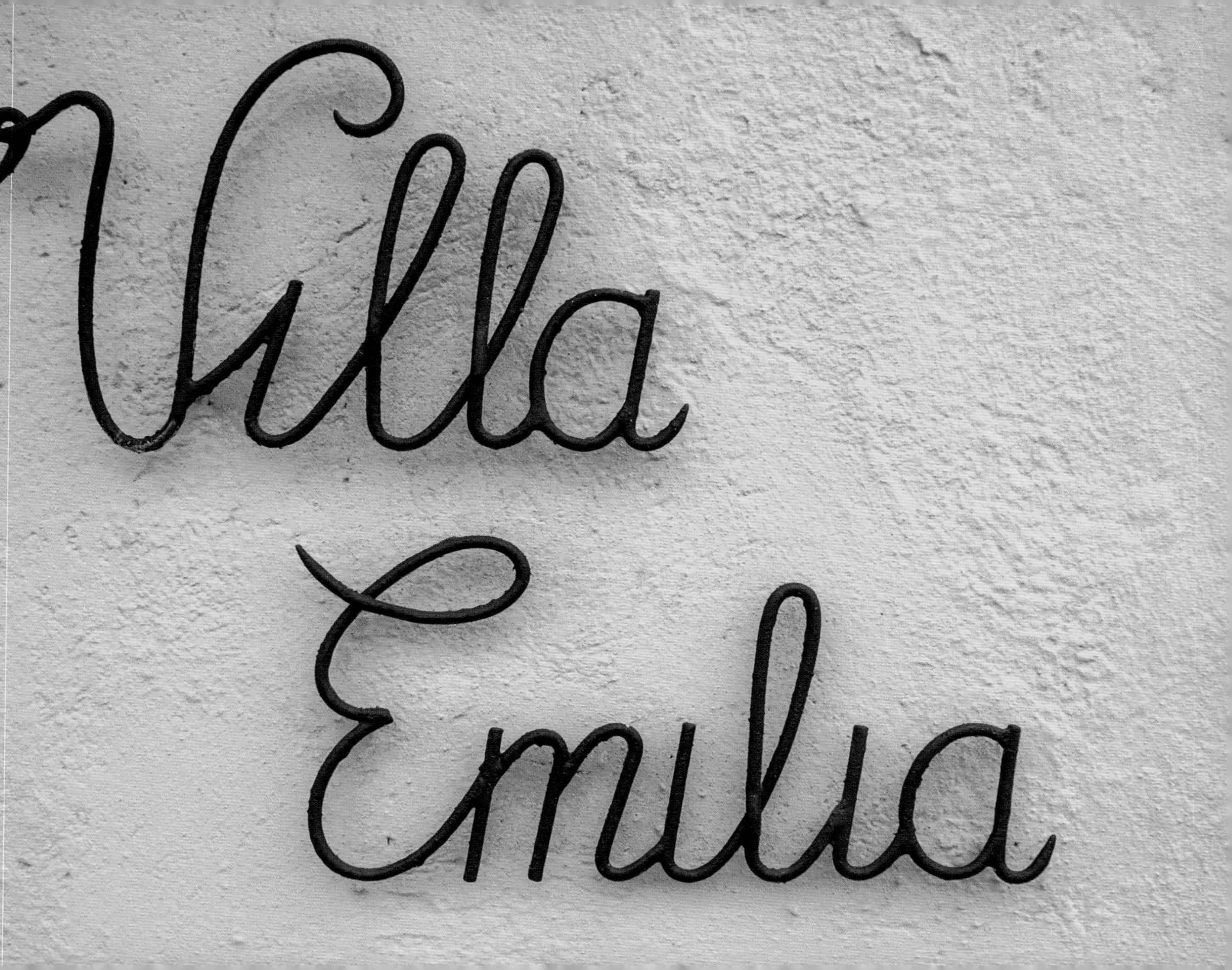
Villa
Emilia

Gambara

El Refugi

Nens i Nenes

la bola

Bomboneria

Limtor.

Mafer

127

Casa Gispert

Fundada l'any 1.851

Productes Sabor

Granja M. Viader
Cardedeu

Central Distribuidora de Manufacturas Textiles, S.A.

— Cedimatexsa —

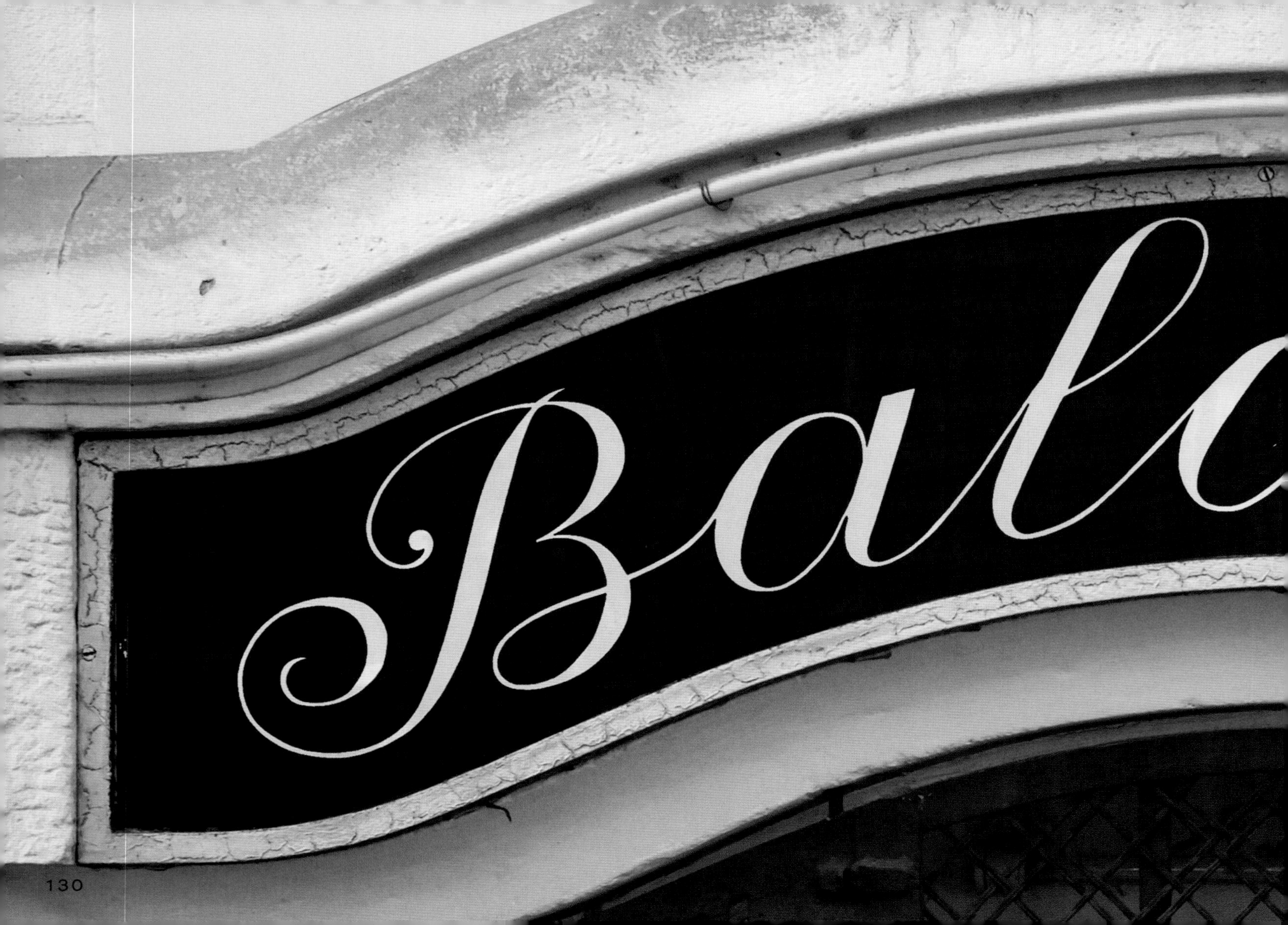
Bal

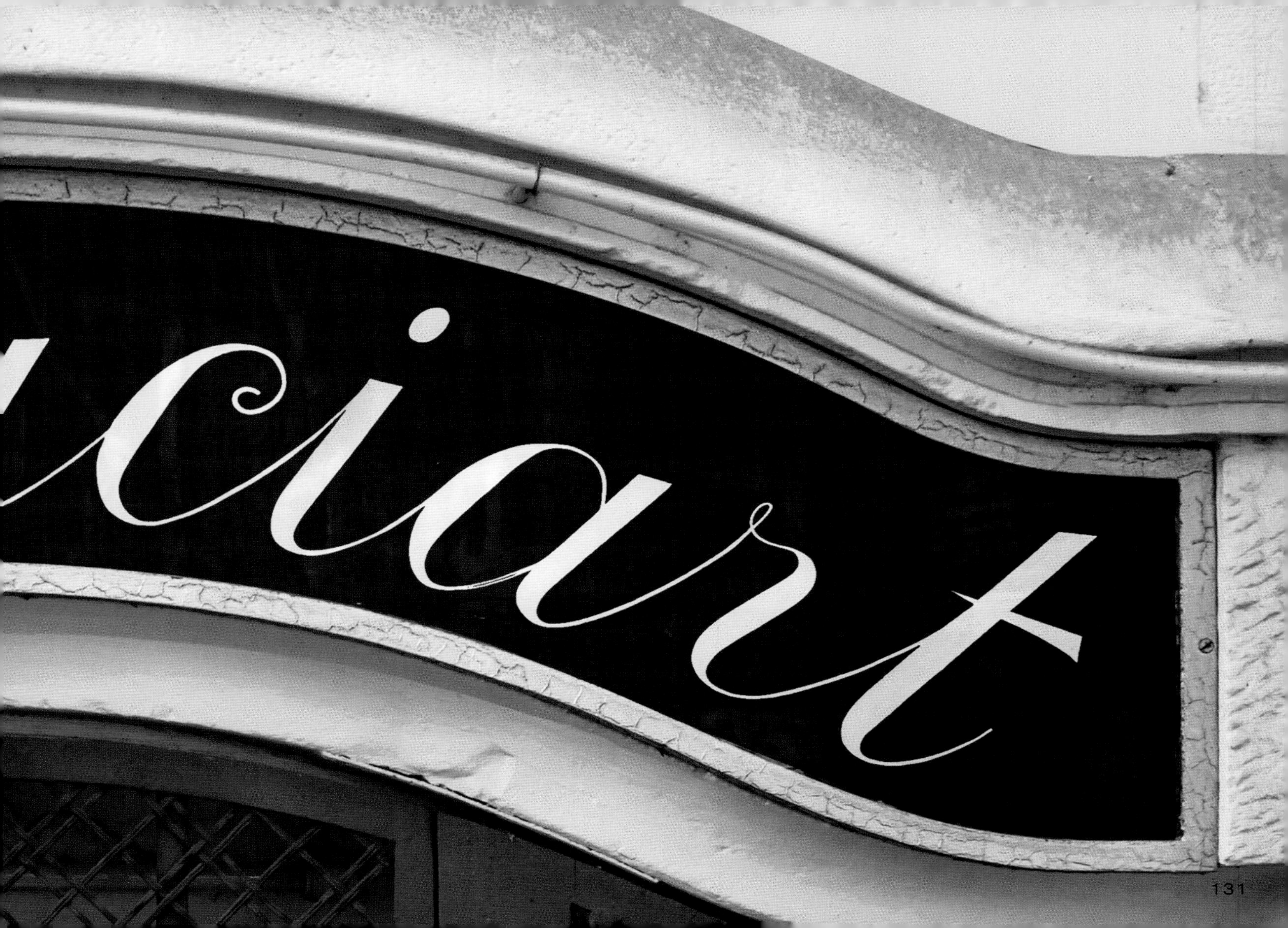
ciart

MOSAICS I VITRALLS

BEAUTIFULLY DISTINCTIVE MOSAICS HAVE BEEN USED TO ADVERTISE AND ENHANCE all types of establishments in Barcelona, from umbrella makers to power plants to concert halls.

Casa Texidor (pages 147–49 and opposite), designed by architect Manuel Joaquim Raspall in 1909, is one of the most magnificent examples. Ornate wrought iron frames this perfectly preserved mosaic sign with gold-outlined uncial lettering on a vividly gradated background, signed by artisan Lluís Bru. Although the space is now home to an optician, the carved wood and stained glass interior recalls the original business, an art supply store, with painted signs (pages 10–11) announcing *Dibujo, Arquitectura,* and *Pintura* (drawing, architecture, and painting).

The stunning mosaic work for Antigua Casa Figueras (pages 144–45) is by the Italian artisan Mario Maragliano, who drew his inspiration from Byzantine ceramic work in Ravenna.

Central Catalana de Electricidad (pages 156–57), a massive brick power station near the Arc de Triomf, was built in 1896. Architect Pere Falqués i Urpí designed an entrance with Modernista type gracefully arched in mosaics. In 1980 the building was converted into offices.

Salve (pages 152–53), Latin for "welcome" or "greetings," is an appropriate salutation to greet the feet that cross the doorway of a side entrance to the Catedral de Barcelona.

Other hard-to-miss mosaics include the side entrance of the Palau de la Música (page 150), with birds playfully positioned on a musical staff, and J. Budesca (page 151), an umbrella workshop where silk and cotton parasols were manufactured starting in 1920.

Leaded glass (*vitralls*) was another popular choice of Modernista artisans. Farmàcia Padrell (pages 166–67), the oldest pharmacy in Barcelona, still maintains its beautiful stained glass sign, originally crafted in 1890 by Joan Espinagosa i Farrando. Farmàcia Enrich, founded in 1902 (page 249), features a stained glass facade, while Farmàcia Bolós (page 165) includes a window with typography that almost seems to be right-reading from both inside and out. Villaplana Vitralls (page 164) still fabricates (and signs) much of the stained glass in Barcelona.

GARAGE

COOPERATIVA O
1901 EL SIG

HORNO-SA

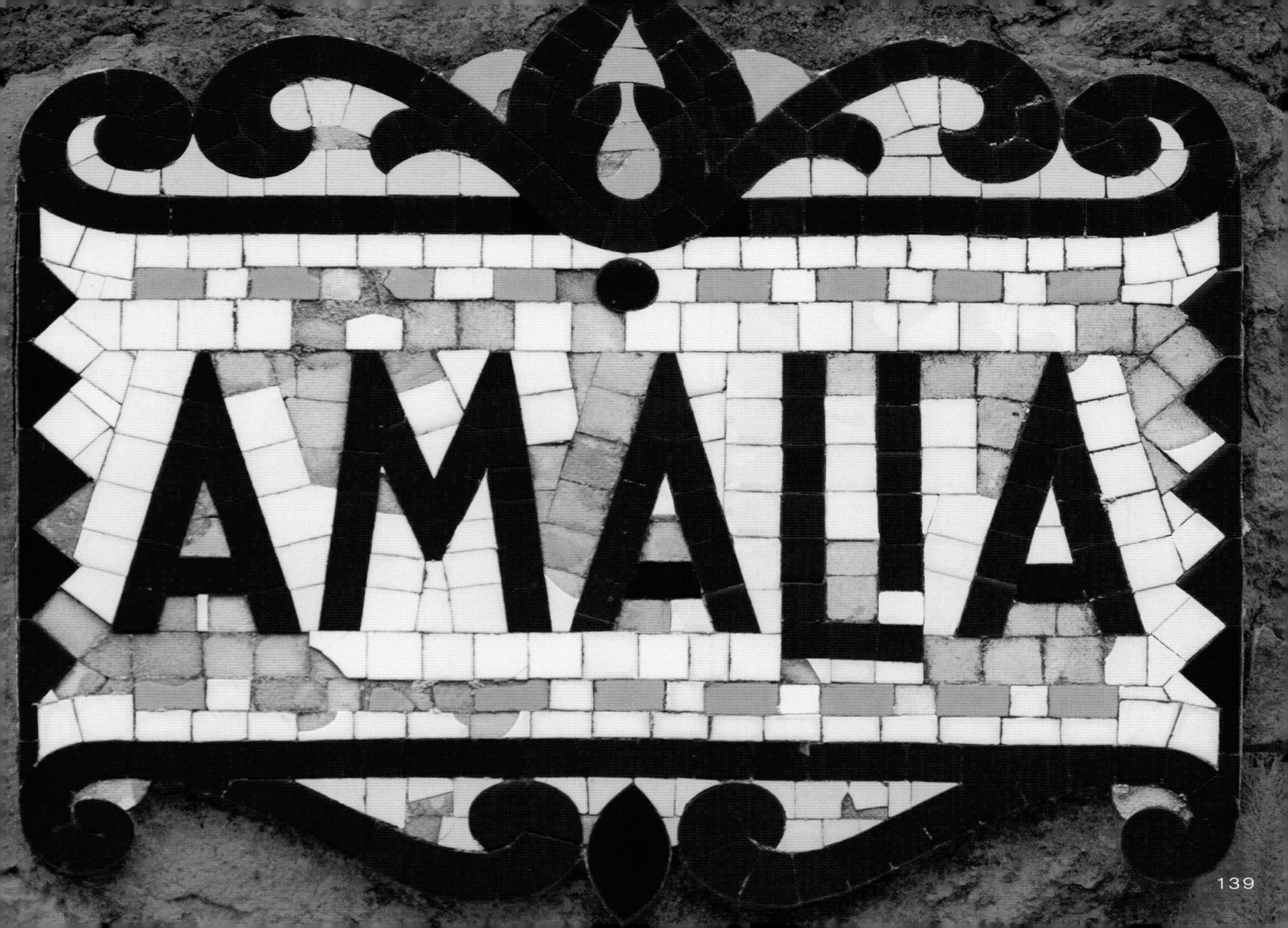
AMALIA

33 FARMACIA

VACUNAS SUEROS LABOR

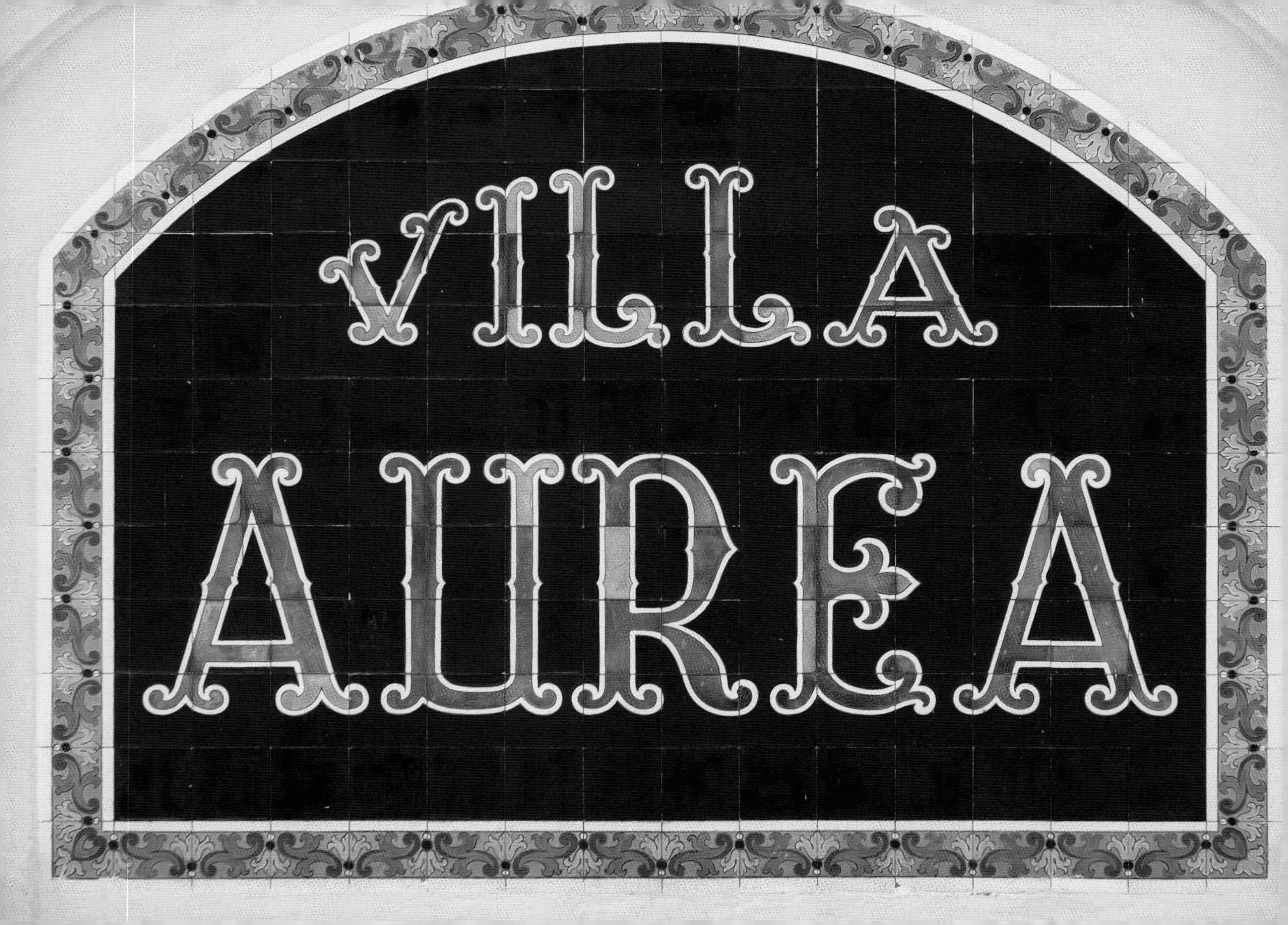
VILLA
AUREA

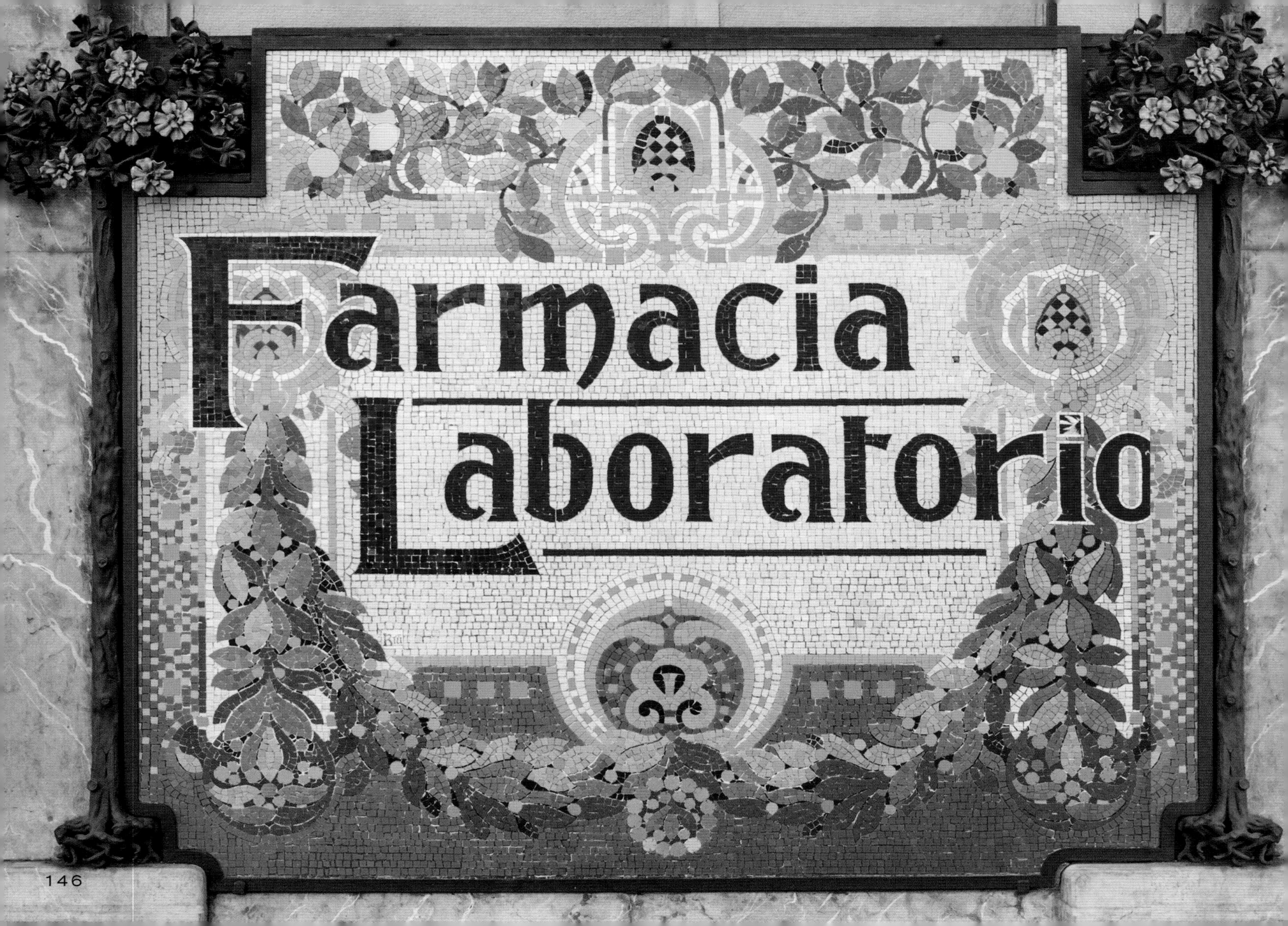
Farmacia
Laboratorio

153

LA PI

TELEF. FIAM

AZUL

257 COMERCI

NEDA

BRES 18505

EJOS

L DERGO 257

FARMACIA
CARMEN

CASELLAS

ARÉS Y HERMANO

DE OLIVA

ECLÈCTIC

IT SHOULD COME AS NO SURPRISE THAT THE WEALTH OF TYPOGRAPHIC STYLES FOUND ON the streets of Barcelona would eventually spawn a spirited generation of letterforms for businesses as varied as electricians and upholsterers. Eclectic typography is as emblematic as its stylistic forebears.

The signs for Pesca Salada F. Mañè (a business that dates back to 1888, page 170) at the Mercat de la Concepció and Ferreteria Rafols (page 171) both employ wrought iron to convey their respective messages (fish and hardware), each in a style that seems to have begun in Modernisme and then found its own aesthetic. Similarly, the letterforms for Ferreri, Hotel Restaurant del Jardí (pages 172–73), and Rincón Galicia (pages 178–79) combine influences of an earlier era.

Casa Gispert, an elegant grocery in El Born, opened in 1851 and still roasts nuts and coffees on the premises. The shop's signage display (pages 176–77) undoubtedly started out in a classical style and has devolved over the years into a hybrid (although still beautiful) version of the original.

Indoor markets in Barcelona can be a veritable breeding ground for eclectic typography. Although many markets have modernized the stalls along with the typography—resulting in lackluster signage—Mercat de l'Abaceria Central in Gràcia (pages 180–81) is one of the few holdouts, with vibrant typographic offerings for the likes of *polleria*, *quesos*, *embutidos*, and *tocineria* (chickens, cheese, sausages, and bacon). In the 1970s Barcelona, like Paris, inexplicably fell under the spell of the idiosyncratic font known as Jackson, with its distinctively top-heavy letterforms (think *Jeopardy* logo). Signs crafted in Jackson and its sibling fonts can be found in much of the market signage.

Cutout letters speak boldly: Tapiceria Vilella (page 182), Ferreteria Llanza (page 183), and Pensión Norma (page 185) not only have exceedingly singular personalities but also appear as though the sign maker enjoyed his work.

The hand-painted type for Arreos de Pesca (pages 178–79) shows off stylish drop shadows. Likewise, the assertive fistful of seemingly animated lightning bolts for J. Torrente Parallamps (pages 174–75) is hard for the passerby to miss.

PESCA

F. MAÑÈ

SALADA

FER

HOTEL
RESTAURANT
DEL JARDÍ

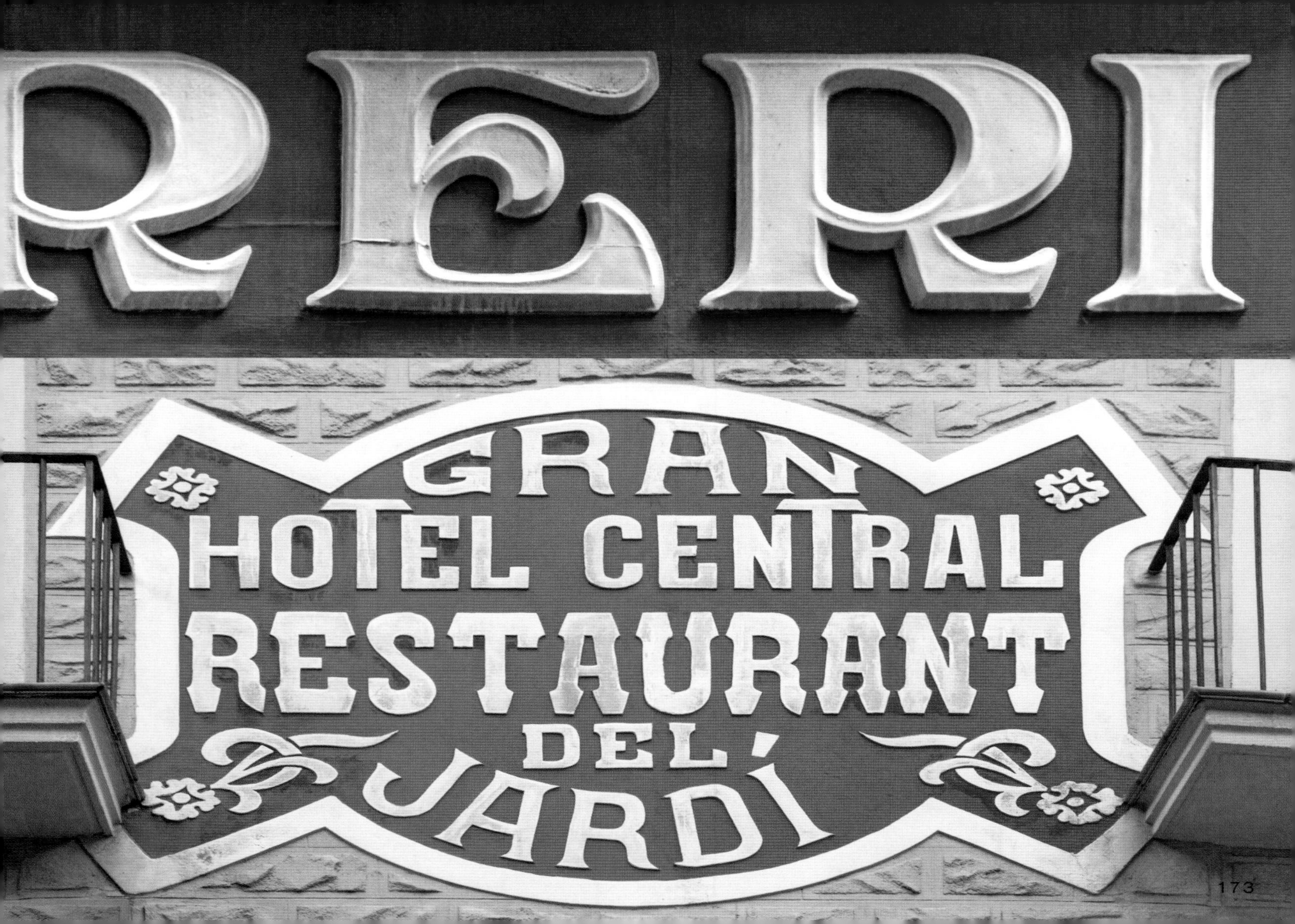
RERI
GRAN
HOTEL CENTRAL
RESTAURANT
DEL
JARDÍ

ELECTRO
MECANICA

J. TOR

MARCA

21 PARAL

ESPECIFICOS

NACIONALES Y EXTRANJEROS

AGUAS

MINERO-MEDICINALES

CAFÉS

COLONIALS

ESPECIES

DIPOSIT DE SAFRA

OXIGENO PURO

ORTOPEDIA

CURA DE LISTER

177

ARREOS de PESCA

RINCON

LA LIONESA

REDES

GALICIA

Vᴰᵃ. ᵈᵉM.VALLES

73 POLLERIA 74

Pollería

QUESOS

POLLERIA y CAZA

EMBUTIDOS
POLLERIA
TOCINERIA
GASCA

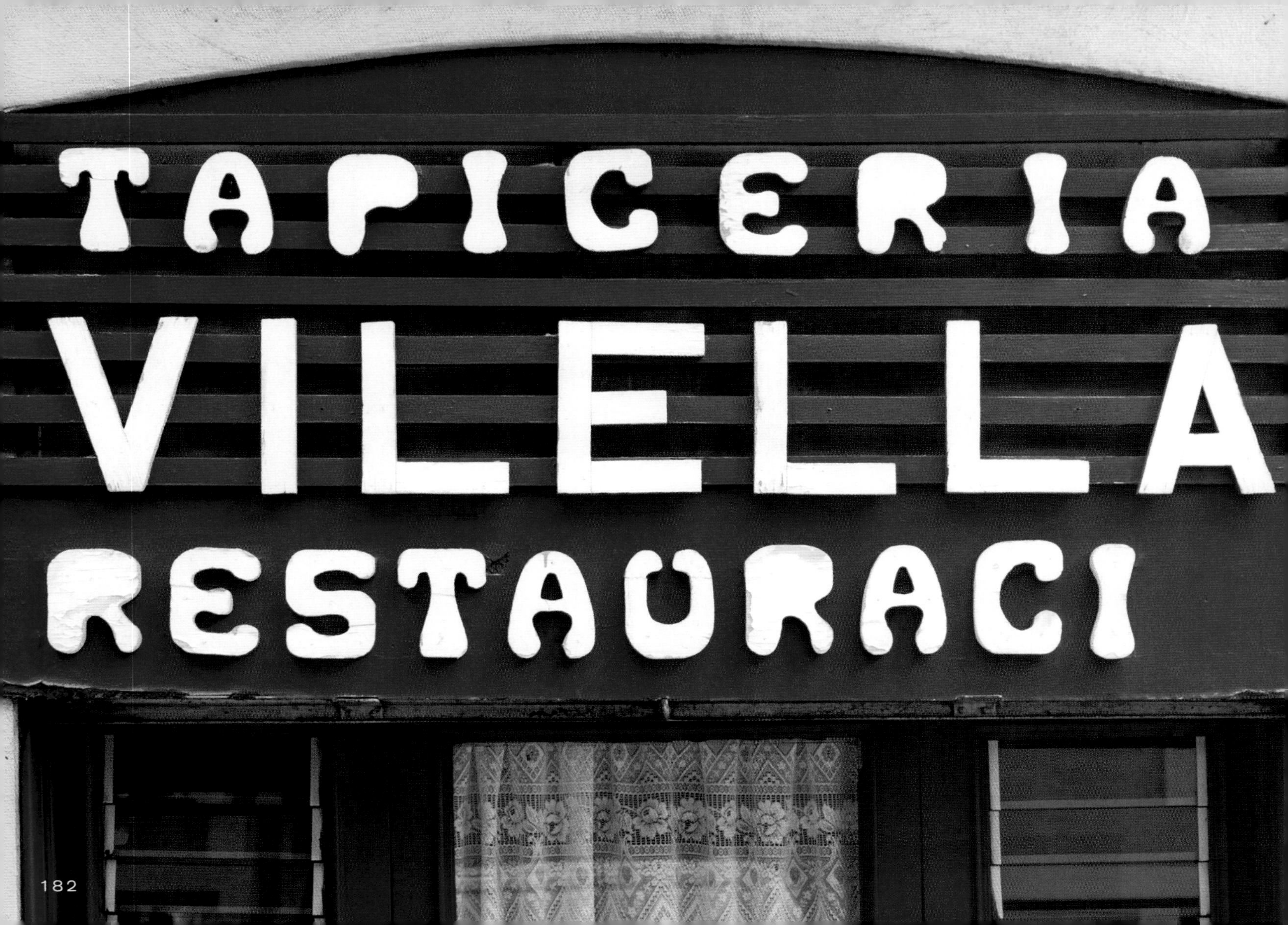
TAPICERIA
VILELLA
RESTAURACI

FERRETERIA
LLANZA

PANADERIA

peluqueria

Paquita

RA

184

PENSION
Norma

Arc Iris

camiseria   roba d'home

MONOGRAMES

THE EIXAMPLE (PRONOUNCED ESH-AM'-PLUH), THE AREA BETWEEN BARCELONA'S old city and what were once surrounding towns, was developed in the late nineteenth and early twentieth centuries. Standing in stark contrast to the cramped, irregular streets of the old city, the strict grid of the Eixample proudly displays much of the city's Modernista architecture, including some of Gaudí's best residential buildings: Casa Milà (nicknamed La Pedrera) and Casa Batlló. The latter is located on the notorious Illa de la Discòrdia (the Block of Discord), named for the visual clash of three buildings by three different architects, each working in the Modernista style. Handsome yet less conspicuous residential buildings followed to populate the neighborhood: the broad, light-filled streets of the Eixample are a showcase for these grand structures, with decorative facades, terraces, and stained glass enclosed balconies.

It is no wonder that the delighted owners of these new buildings in the late 1800s wanted everyone in the neighborhood to know who lived there. It is therefore impossible to walk down a block in the Eixample without coming across one striking monogram after another, each bearing the initials of the family who resided there (and may still).

These typographic gems, usually consisting of two or more overlapping letters, are located on the main facades just above the entrance and are a graceful nod to another era. Often the monogram is paired with the year (or years) of construction, examples of which can be seen in the Arquitectònic chapter (pages 218–43).

Sculpted magnificently in stone or plaster, monograms can also be found crafted in wrought iron, cut out of sheet metal, and occasionally gilded (opposite).

The *JG* monogram on page 216 (top right) is located above the door of the former home of Josep Guardiola, a local who made his fortune in the Guatemalan coffee trade. After her husband's death, Guardiola's widow, Roser Segimon i Artrells, married Pere Milà i Camps, who commisioned Gaudí to build Casa Milà, a few steps away on the Passeig de Gràcia. With its undulating stone facade and elaborate wrought iron balconies, Casa Milà lacks nothing—except perhaps a monogram.

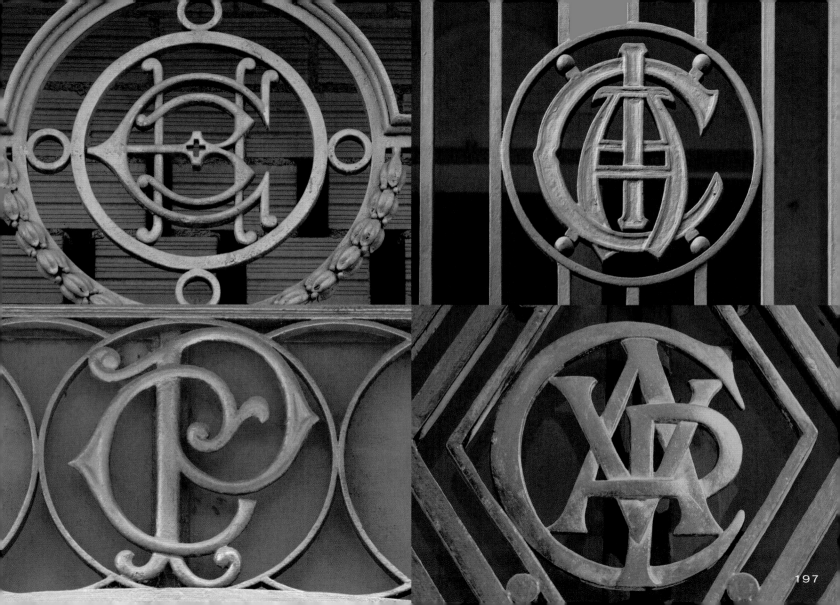

ARQUITECTÒNIC

S EVIDENCED IN THE PREVIOUS CHAPTER, ARCHITECTS HAD A PROFOUND INFLUENCE on the typographic landscape of Barcelona, using materials, thankfully, with staying power.

Building owners wanted the general public (and future generations) to be well informed of the date of construction, which was announced on facades with great fanfare, fitting inventively into ovals and keystone shapes or displayed in a series of elegant angled compositions (page 224). The year was often listed on its own or preceded by *Año* or *Any* (Spanish and Catalan, respectively, for "year").

Barcelona architects explored every possible way of creatively combining four numerals: consider *1908* with a nine gracefully threaded through a zero (page 232) or *1924* with nestled figures that seem somewhat aquatic (page 220). Sometimes the numerals were treated like monograms, with all four figures intersecting (page 234), which, although charming, can be challenging to decode.

Wrought iron provided another medium for architects to mark the time. In countless examples found around the city—each different from the next—lacy scrollwork gracefully frames the centrally sited numerals (pages 228–29). In the late 1800s it was the fashion in some European countries to interpret the numeral *1* to look more like an uppercase *J*; crafting the number like this in wrought iron was particularly appropriate for better readability.

Building numbers in Barcelona are varied and unique, rendered in enamel, mosaic, or wrought iron; hand-painted; or cut out of metal. Casa Calvet, one of Gaudí's first buildings, was commissioned by a textile manufacturer for use as a residence (on the upper floors) and business (on the ground floor—now a restaurant). The columns at the entrance were designed as stacks of bobbins to reference the nature of his business. The unmistakably Gaudí-designed building number is on the facing page, while his gold-leafed *1899* is on page 231.

It is only appropriate that after giving such care to outfitting building facades for posterity, the architect gets to take a bow. If you set your gaze a little higher along the urban vista of Barcelona, you will occasionally find the maker's imprimatur (page 243) bestowing credit where it is well due.

227

7 Y 9

AÑO 1889

75

242

J. BOADA BARBA

-ARQTE.-

F. NEBOT

ARQTO.

SENSE PARAULES

I N   B A R C E L O N A ,   W H E R E   S O   M U C H   C A N   B E   S A I D   A B O U T   S O   M A N Y   T H I N G S ,   T H E R E   A R E   actually times when silence is appropriate. For shops selling eyeglasses, for example, words are unnecessary. An optician needs nothing more than a pair of spectacles mounted perpendicular to the shop facade to communicate its message. Signs *sense paraules*, or without words, speak volumes—in neon, wood, or even boldly painted onto a door grating (opposite). This approach is nothing new. In centuries past, this was the most efficient way for a merchant to connect with an often illiterate public.

The Maltese cross, the design of which is based on crosses used since the First Crusade, is distinguished by eight outward points, and traditionally symbolized hospitality and care. Many of Barcelona's *farmàcies* adopted a stylized version of the cross, with flatter sides. City ordinance number 168, from 1990, indicates that the crosses should be red, although green is also permitted. The crosses make prominent appearances in neon, hand-painted on wood, and on blinking LED panels. The dimensional cross paired with wrought iron (page 250, bottom right) is positioned on the distinctive corner facade of Farmàcia Nadal (pages 46–47).

In addition to the cross, the pharmaceutical caduceus is another symbol widely used by *farmàcies* and is represented by a snake coiled around a cup (page 247, left, and pages 248–49). The snake symbolizes healing art, fertility, and life. The cup belongs to Hygeia, daughter of Asclepius and goddess of health, whose custom was to drink to the snake of the temple of Asclepius at Epidaurus. The symbol has been interpreted in every imaginable material: stained glass, gold leaf, mosaics, marble—from classic to modern.

The (nonpharmaceutical) caduceus (page 246, left, and page 247, right) represents success in business, commerce, and transportation, and is derived from the god Hermes. It was widely used as a symbol for progress.

And finally, let us not overlook the salute to cute: wrought iron and stained glass (page 254) make a memorable and wordless sign for restaurant Los Caracoles (The Snails). And a carved bee, wrought iron peacock, or stylized flower (page 255) will make any passerby stop and smile.

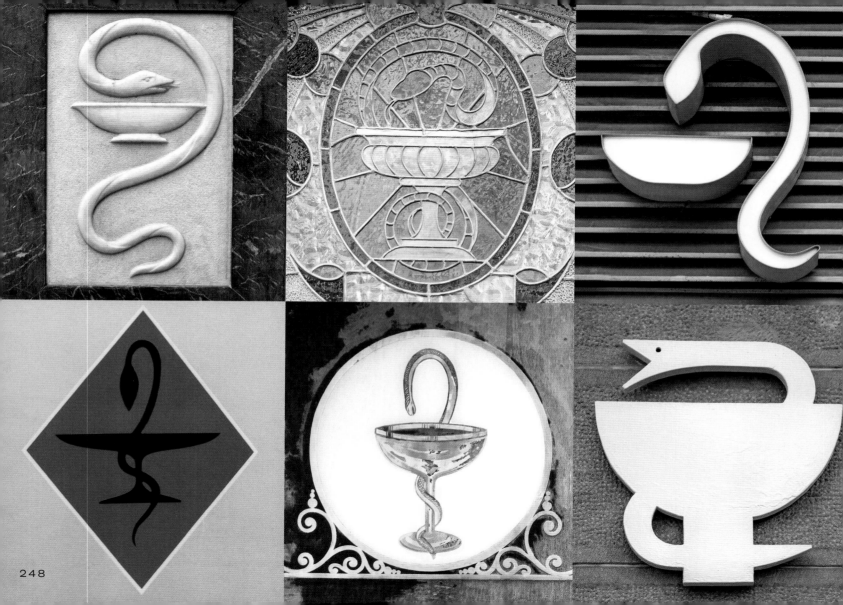

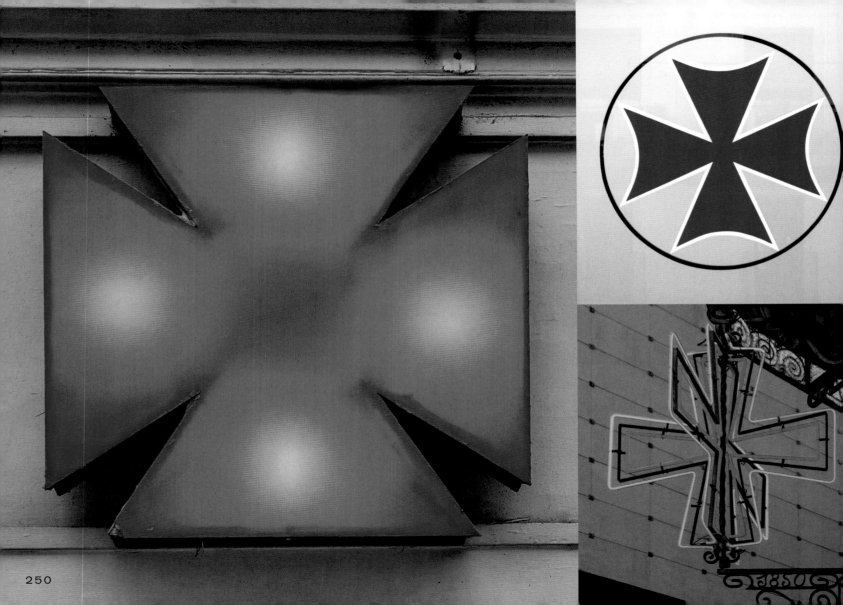

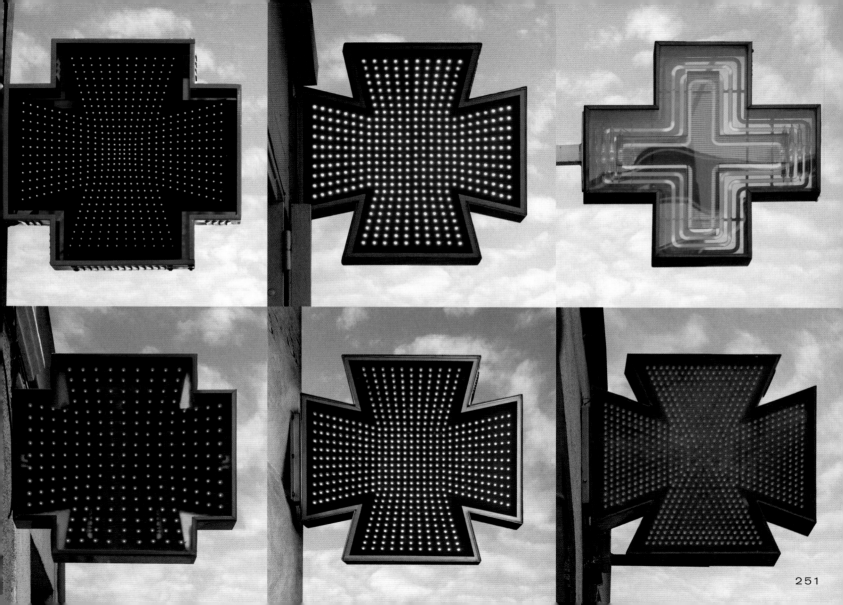

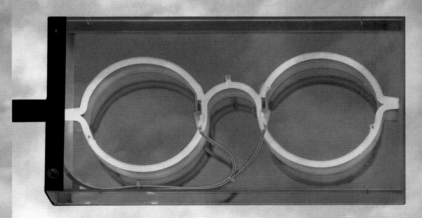

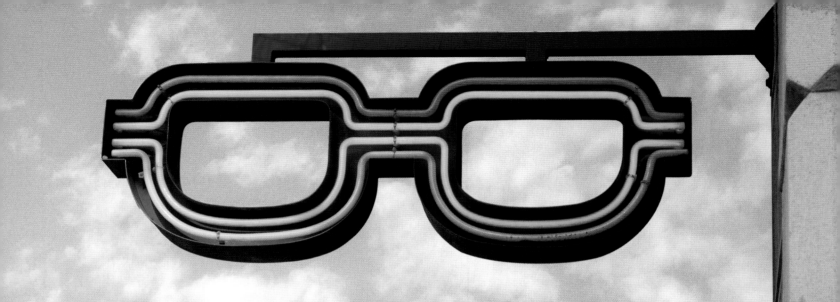

BARCELONA, JANUARY 2016

MOSAICS I VITRALLS

198: AA
Ronda de Sant Pere, 27

198: PLL/1889
Carrer de Consell de Cent, 281

199: A/R
Carrer d'Ausiàs Marc, 20

200: FS
Passeig de Sant Joan, 80

200: EG
Carrer del Brosolí, 1

200: J
Carrer de Muntaner, 34

200: RH
Carrer de Roger de Llúria, 30

201: EM
Carrer d'Aribau, 11

202: JC
Carrer de Casp, 41

203: PPL
Carrer de València, 195

203: B
Ronda de la Universitat, 24

203: VJ
Carrer d'Ausiàs Marc, 29

203: MB
Carrer de Pau Clarís, 117

204: A/R/F/C
Rambla de Catalunya, 71

205: AD
Passeig de Sant Joan, 110

206: CB
Rambla de Catalunya, 11

207: JB
Rambla de Catalunya, 75

207: JM
Carrer de Mallorca, 200

208: J.P.F.
Carrer del Bonaire, 7

209: MP
Carrer de Pere IV, 60

210: B
Carrer d'Ausiàs Marc, 48

210: AM
Carrer de Balmes, 54

210: B
Carrer de la Diputació, 246

210: B
Carrer de Casp, 44

211: FVL
Passeig de Gràcia, 114

212: R&P
Carrer de Consell de Cent, 280

213: T&S
Carrer del Carme, 8
This monogram appears on the elaborate mosaic facade of Farmàcia del Carmen (pages 158–59).

214: AS
Carrer de Casp, 46

214: FN
Plaça de la Universitat, 5

215: GI
Rambla de Catalunya, 13

215: SR
Carrer Gran de Gràcia, 7

216: AE
Carrer d'Enric Granados, 7

216: SM
Ronda de Sant Antoni, 41
St. Moritz has been bottling its famous Catalan beer on the premises since 1856. Note the hops in the background of the monogram design.

216: JG
Passatge de la Concepció, 4

216: B
Carrer de Còrsega, 286

217: A
Rambla de Catalunya, 125

217: VC
Rambla de Catalunya, 31

217: A
Carrer del Notariat, 11

217: AR
Carrer de Balmes, 23

ARQUITECTÒNIC

219: 48
Casa Calvet
Carrer de Casp, 48

220: 1924
Carrer de Bailèn, 89

220: 1891
Carrer de la Diputació, 187

220: 1881
Gran Via de les Corts Catalanes, 663

221: 1909
Passeig de Gràcia, 117

221: 1897
Carrer de Muntaner, 104

221: 1901
Passeig de Gràcia, 115

222: Salve/Mater
Avinguda Diagonal, 422

223: 1896
Carrer de Roger de Llúria, 83

224: 1886
Carrer de Bruc, 26

224: 1887
Carrer de Bruc, 28

224: 1888
Carrer de Bruc, 32

224: 1892/1893
Carrer de Mallorca, 202

225: 1902
Carrer Ali Bei, 27

225: 1902
Carrer de Girona, 1

226: 207
Carrer de València, 207

227: 1889
Carrer de la Diputació, 353

SENSE PARAULES

The panot *design featured on the copyright page is a Catalan icon found on tiles throughout Barcelona. It is based on one of the most familiar versions of the* panot, *the "Flor de Barcelona," introduced in 1926.*

GRÀCIES

I AM GRATEFUL TO PRINCETON ARCHITECTURAL PRESS FOR THEIR SUPPORT: PUBLISHER KEVIN Lippert, editorial director Jennifer Lippert, editor Sara Stemen, production director Janet Behning, and art director Paul Wagner. Also to Tanya Heinrich for copyediting.

In Barcelona, my deepest gratitude goes to my friend Jordi Duró, without whose generosity and enthusiasm this book would not have been possible. Jordi's introductions to all the right people made all the difference: Cristian Segura, whose insightful article in *El País* led to the discovery of an unattainable sign, and Carla Cimino, who helped me navigate the often confusing streets, cheerfully asking shop owners to open (or close) awnings or to turn lights on (or off) for this non-Catalan speaker. Thank you to the entire López family of Fotos López, especially Angel López, for his kind offer to temporarily remount the sign for his family's photo studio so that I might photograph it. I am indebted to America Sanchez and Enric Satué, whose early publications on Barcelona signage provided a great impetus to pursue my own books on Italian and Parisian signs. Also to Tarek Atrissi, Marc Marti, Laura Meseguer, Victor Oliva, and Òscar Dalmau. Several Instagram feeds have offered continued inspiration: omarstudio, barcelona_type, agencia_próteccion_tipografica, and letrerosbcn.

In New York, immense thanks to my staff at Louise Fili Ltd: Nicholas Misani, Raphael Geroni, and Rachel Michaud for their expert design and Photoshop work, in addition to Nick's masterful work on the cover and Raphael's maps. Thanks to Kelly Thorn and Spencer Charles for their suggestions and to Ted Palenski for his invaluable help with the title. To James Clough, for his always sage advice, and Marcia Lippman and Beth Tondreau, for their recommendations. Thank you to Adobe Systems for the Fujifilm camera that made my work so much more enjoyable. Once again, Google Street View was a significant time-saver and allowed me hours of blissfully wandering the Barcelona streets while sitting at my desk in New York.

Finally, my love and gratitude to my family, Nicolas Heller and Steven Heller, for patiently accompanying me on yet another picture-taking odyssey.